Innkeepers' Best

Cookies

60 Delicious Recipes Shared by
Bed & Breakfast Innkeepers
Across the Country

Laura Zahn

Down to Earth Publications

Published by
Down to Earth Publications
1032 West Montana Avenue
St. Paul, MN 55117

ISBN 0-939301-57-1

Printed in the USA

99 00 01 02 03 5 4 3 2 1

Cover photo credit: Fudge Mound Cookies (recipe, page 55), photo courtesy of The Gosby House, Pacific Grove, California, owned by the Four Sisters Inns, Monterey, California.

Cover and interior design by Helene C. J. Anderson, Stillwater, Minnesota

To order additional copies by mail, send a check or money order for $12.95 each to Down to Earth Publications, 1032 W. Montana Ave., St. Paul, MN 55117 (includes shipping by 4th class mail). If you wish UPS delivery, send a check for $13.95 and include a street address (no P.O. boxes). To charge your order with a Visa or MasterCard, call 800-585-6211 or fax 651-488-7862.

Introduction

*H*omemade cookies. *Mmmm,* just say that and close your eyes and you can smell them baking. What else is there that we fall in love with at age two or three and continue to crave and covet for the rest of our lives? Over what else could a blue, furry character on a popular public TV show for children routinely lose control and gobble madly? What else invokes some of the most pleasant memories of childhood? A good homemade cookie is the perfect embodiment of what B&B inns offer: created with attention to detail and offered in the spirit of hospitality and comfort. It's no wonder that a large hotel chain makes a big deal out of giving "homemade" chocolate chip cookies to its guests. But small B&Bs and inns, where guests can often smell those cookies baking, are the most appropriate setting for that "Grandma's House" kind of feeling a full cookie jar evokes.

Successful innkeepers out there are often pressing their heavy-duty mixers into service, whipping up batch after batch of traditional recipes and new favorites to please their guests. Guests checking in might find them waiting in their rooms, placed on a pretty plate and covered with plastic wrap. Or they might be offered as a bedtime snack in the dining room. Or there might be a raid-the-cookie-jar invitation anytime day or night. One of the inns in the book, Thorwood and Rosewood Inns in Hastings, MN, even sends guests off with a "journey cake," a delicious wrapped almond cookie, which they receive at check-out.

Lucky for us, innkeepers were willing to share recipes! Some sent recipes that their grandmothers or ancestors before them began making. Others concocted new treats to use regional specialties or use up a surplus of a particular ingredient. Some passed on recipes that had been passed on to them. Whatever the story behind them, we gratefully received them and hope you, too, will treasure and enjoy them.

Here are a few tips for making great cookies:

- If you don't have insulated cookie sheets, run, don't walk, to your nearest bakeware store and get two or three. They are worth the investment — unless you *really* overbake them, you won't burn your cookies on the bottom again.
- To keep cookies "fat" and from spreading too much, chill the dough before baking for a half hour or more.
- Always cool the cookies on the pan, on a cake rack, for at least a few minutes before eating or removing them to cool completely on a clean countertop or tabletop. Some, like shortbreads, don't keep long, so indulge right away!
- Most cookies do benefit from a cookie sheet that's been at least lightly-greased with shortening or non-stick cooking spray.
- If you make a lot of cookies, consider investing in a heavy duty mixer. Hand-held mixers and "light weights" can't beat a thick cookie dough without burning out the motor.

"Inn-dulge!"

– Laura Zahn

CONTENTS

Cookie Recipes ■ 7 to 125

Thorwood and Rosewood Inns

*T*he year was 1983, and in Minnesota, hardly anyone had heard of B&Bs, let alone stayed in one. That was the year that Pam and Dick Thorsen opened two guestrooms in their 1880 home. They had bought the apartment building for their home and to generate a little extra income. But it turned out the Thorsens were perfect for the B&B business: Dick is quite capable of undertaking major historic restoration projects and Pam, the consummate romantic, decorates luxurious suites and entices guests to them. Today they own and operate two historic inns with a total of 15 guestrooms, and the popular inns are often named Minnesota's best and most-romantic getaways. Thorwood, as it is now named, was built as a lumber baron's home in this Mississippi rivertown. Eventually, it was turned into a private hospital and then an apartment house. After unending work, it now has seven guestrooms on three floors, all with fireplaces and/or whirlpools. In 1986, they purchased another historic home that once served as a hospital. Rosewood, owned by the city and in disrepair, was "gutted" to the studs and rebuilt with eight luxurious suites and a gift shop on the back porch. Guests can sequester themselves in luxury, ordering hat box suppers on the weekends, or breakfast served in their suites or in formal dining spaces. Or they can stroll downtown for dinner and coffee. Located only a half-hour from St. Paul, Hastings has a winery, nature center, antique stores, two coffee shops, a toy store, a Scandinavian shop, and a well-loved restaurant, all in town or nearby.

Pam, who is active in historic preservation efforts in the city, creates several special packages and theme weekends. Learn more on the Web, www.thorwoodinn.com

Thorwood and Rosewood Inns

315 Pine Street
Hastings, MN 55033
651-437-3297 ■ *Fax 651-437-4129*

Ann's Famous Chocolate Chip Cookies

"These cookies from one of our employees, Ann, are famous around here," said Innkeeper Pam Thorsen. "Guests can't even taste the coconut, but know that the cookies are fabulously moist because of it." The recipe is doubled when it's made for the cookie jars at Thorwood and Rosewood. Makes 3 dozen cookies.

   1 cup butter-flavored shortening
   ¾ cup sugar
   ¾ cup brown sugar, packed
   1 teaspoon vanilla extract
   2 eggs
   2½ cups flour
   ½ cup coconut
   1 teaspoon baking soda
   1 teaspoon salt
   ½ cup semi-sweet chocolate chips

- With an electric mixer, cream shortening, sugar and brown sugar.
- Beat in vanilla and the eggs, one at a time, scraping bowl after each addition.
- In a separate bowl, stir together flour, coconut, baking soda and salt.
- Beat flour mixture slowly into sugar mixture. Stir in chocolate chips by hand.
- If batter is too sticky to roll into balls, add more coconut or flour.
- Preheat oven to 350 degrees.
- Roll batter into balls the size of golf balls. Place on greased cookie sheets and bake for 10 minutes or until set.
- Remove from oven and cool for a few minutes before removing cookies.

Apple Gate Bed & Breakfast

*S*easonal fresh fruit is always a part of breakfast at the Apple Gate, and that includes fresh berries from a neighbor's organic farm, as well as apples, of course. Because Apple Gate is located just across the street from a ninety-acre apple orchard, Innkeeper Dianne Legenhausen chose an apple motif to decorate the inn, including naming the four guestrooms after apple varieties. Even Dianne and Ken's one hundred-pound yellow lab, Mac, is named after the Macintosh apple (the cat, Jessie, however, was acquired before the inn and has no apple ties).

Before innkeeping, Dianne taught music to elementary-age children and Ken was a police officer specializing in emergency rescues. While they had many friends in Long Island, New York, where they lived and worked for many years, they decided to head for the Monadnock region of New Hampshire, said to be picture-perfect Currier and Ives country, for their second careers as innkeepers.

They found this 1832 Colonial home just two miles from downtown Peterborough. It offered spacious accommodations for guests, including a double parlor, where guests may enjoy a fire, the library, or a TV and collection of videos. Peterborough is home to the Sharon Arts Center, and the Legenhausen's bed-and-breakfast is just a few miles from the Temple Mountain and Windblown ski areas.

Apple Gate Bed & Breakfast
199 Upland Road
Peterborough, NH 03458
603-924-6543

Apple Harvest Cookies

"I fill a glass pumpkin jar with these cookies every fall," said Innkeeper Dianne Legenhausen. "And if my husband Ken hasn't gotten to them first, they are a wonderful treat to welcome guests back from their autumn walk. In the words of one of our guests, 'these cookies taste like fall!'" Makes 6 dozen cookies.

½   cup butter
1¼ cups brown sugar, firmly packed
1   egg
2   cups flour
1   teaspoon baking soda
1   teaspoon cinnamon
1   teaspoon cloves
½   teaspoon nutmeg
½   teaspoon salt
1   cup apples, peeled, cored and chopped finely
1   cup raisins
1   cup chopped walnuts
¼   cup milk

■ Preheat oven to 400 degrees. Grease cookie sheets.
■ With an electric mixer, cream the butter, brown sugar and egg.
■ In a separate bowl, sift together the flour, baking soda, cinnamon, cloves, nutmeg and salt.
■ Beat flour mixture into creamed mixture.
■ Stir in apples, raisins, walnuts and milk by hand, blending well.
■ Drop dough by teaspoonfuls onto the greased cookie sheets.
■ Bake for 12 to 15 minutes or until cookie is "set."

The Woods House Bed & Breakfast

*J*n the spring of 1991, Françoise and Lester Roddy moved from Berkeley, California, and purchased the Woods House Bed and Breakfast, which has been in existence since 1984. Françoise previously worked in human resources and event planning and brought calligraphy, cooking, needlecraft, and gardening skills to the innkeeping business; Lester brought over 25 years of business management.

Both innkeepers enjoy creating taste treats for their guests, such as fresh peach pie. The Roddys also enjoy setting up theme weekends. The inn hosts popular "murder mystery weekends" at Valentine's Day, Halloween, and New Year's Eve; and in the spring and fall, they host workshops for aspiring innkeepers.

The Woods House breakfasts feature local produce, when in season, in such yummy dishes as Miz Jasmine's Sweet Onion Pie, named in honor of the "friendly Newfie" Jasmine who lives at the Woods House and encourages dog-walking at every turn. Other delicious items are blueberry oatmeal pancakes, wild rice buckwheat pancakes with cranberry butter, and, of course, freshly baked muffins and scones.

Nearby are hiking and biking trails, river rafting, golf, horseback riding, wineries, marvelous bookstores, community theaters and the renowned Oregon Shakespeare Festival. The Woods' half acre of terraced English gardens is shaded by majestic trees and abounds with flowers and herbs and quiet places for guests to relax. The 1908 Craftsman-style inn has six guestrooms, and is just four and one-half blocks from the downtown plaza. Learn more on the Web, www.mind.net/woodshouse/

The Woods House Bed & Breakfast

333 North Main Street
Ashland, OR 97520
541-488-1598
Fax 541-482-8027

Banana Lemon Bars with Chocolate Chips

"Here is a very quick, easy and yummy bar that uses up too-ripe-to-eat bananas and does not require eggs," notes Innkeeper Françoise Roddy. Her guests appreciate having these treats waiting for them when they return from outdoor theater during the summer or from skiing, rafting or hiking in the area. Makes 21 to 24 bars.

- 1 cup brown sugar, packed
- ¼ cup butter-flavored shortening
- ½ teaspoon vanilla extract
- ½ teaspoon lemon extract
- 1 cup mashed, very ripe banana (2 to 3 bananas)
- 1½ cups flour
- 1½ teaspoons baking powder
- ½ teaspoon salt
- ½ cup chopped nuts
- ½ cup semi-sweet chocolate chips

Coating
- ⅓ cup powdered sugar
- 1 teaspoon cinnamon

- ■ Preheat oven to 350 degrees. Grease an 11 x 7-inch pan.
- ■ In a mixing bowl, beat brown sugar, shortening, vanilla, lemon extract, and bananas until well-mixed.
- ■ Sift flour with baking powder and salt. Add to banana-shortening mixture and mix well.
- ■ Stir in nuts and chocolate chips.
- ■ Pour into pan. Bake for 30 to 35 minutes or until a toothpick inserted in the center comes out clean (unless you stab a chocolate chip!).
- ■ Cut the bars while still warm and remove from pan.
- ■ For coating, mix powdered sugar and cinnamon. Gently roll around the warm bars in the mixture until all sides are coated.

Martin Oaks Bed & Breakfast

*I*n 1990, Marie Vogl Gery and husband Frank bought this home, listed on the National Register of Historic Places and located on the Cannon River. The first portion of Sara Etta Archibald Martin's home was built in 1855, just a few years after her brothers and cousin founded the town of Dundas; the "addition," where the three guestrooms are located, was constructed in 1869. Rooms are designed to take guests back into the romance and elegance of the past. High beds have down pillows and comforters. And there's always a bedtime treat: brownies, brandy snaps, or fresh fruit.

Guests of Martin Oaks dine on fine china by candlelight, and breakfast always includes homebaked breads or muffins, an entrée, and dessert. Enjoy blueberry muffins with blueberry filling, lemon yogurt Bundt cakes, fresh basil omelettes, spicy pepper eggs or Martin Oaks Signature French Toast with meringue topping.

Marie and Frank encourage guests to take the historic walking tour through this town of 422 or relax on the veranda or in the parlor. Some choose to read *The Mystery of the House with Four Stairs,* a delightful story about this house written half a century ago. Marie, a professional storyteller, can fill visitors in on both past and present.

Martin Oaks B&B

107 First Street
P.O. Box 207
Dundas, MN 55019
507-645-4644

Brandy Snaps

"My Aunt Marie kept a wee bottle of brandy on hand for medicinal purposes, and for Brandy Snaps," said Innkeeper Marie Gery. "Her secret was the addition of orange or lemon rind — it adds a bit more taste." Makes 24 cookies.

$\frac{1}{2}$ cup butter (not margarine)
$\frac{1}{2}$ cup sugar
$\frac{1}{3}$ cup molasses
$\frac{1}{4}$ teaspoon ginger
$\frac{1}{2}$ teaspoon cinnamon
$\frac{1}{2}$ teaspoon grated orange peel
1 cup flour
2 teaspoons brandy
semi-sweet chocolate chips, optional

Filling

1 cup whipping cream
3 tablespoons powdered sugar
$\frac{1}{2}$ teaspoon vanilla extract

- Preheat oven to 325 degrees. If you like, spray cookie sheets with non-stick cooking spray and top with parchment, but do not grease cookie sheets.
- In a saucepan over low heat, stir together the butter, sugar, molasses, ginger, cinnamon, and orange peel. Stir until sugar is no longer visible. Remove from heat and stir in the flour and brandy. Chill in the refrigerator for 30 minutes.
- Roll dough into $\frac{3}{4}$-inch balls. Bake on cookie sheet, one cookie sheet at a time, for 10 to 12 minutes.
- Remove from oven and let cookies cool a bit. Then quickly roll each lacy cookie around the handle of a wooden spoon, leaving them on the spoon until the cookie can hold its shape. (Briefly rewarm the cookies in the oven if necessary.)
- You may decide to give each cookie a filling, and dip it in melted chocolate!
- For the filling, whip the cream until stiff. Beat in the powdered sugar and vanilla extract. Fill each cookie with mixture. (Filling is optional.)
- For another option, melt some chocolate chips in a microwave-safe bowl in the microwave, stirring frequently, until smooth. Dip an end of each curled brandy snap into the chocolate. Place the dipped cookies on waxed paper. Let cool.

Window on the Winds

*L*eanne McClain's two-story log home is the perfect base for a Wyoming vacation. The second floor, with four guestrooms featuring lodgepole pine beds, is reserved for guests. A view of the Wind River Mountains from the fireside gathering room has been known to take more than one guest's breath away.

Leanne is an archeologist who enjoys sharing her perspective on the area and can offer information about the history of the Green River Basin and the Wind River Range. She is also happy to help guests plan their fishing, rafting, riding, skiing, or hiking adventures.

Window on the Winds is located directly on the Continental Divide Snowmobile Trail at elevation 7,175 feet. A guided inn-to-inn snowmobile tour that leads into Yellowstone National Park leaves right from the property. Guests can snowmobile from the front door, through the Wind River Mountains and on into Yellowstone National Park. Other winter adventures include dog sledding and racing, and both cross-country and downhill skiing.

Whatever the season, guests can return from a day of outdoor adventure to relax and enjoy the hot tub. Fresh fruits, vegetables, and whole grains are always on the breakfast menu. Leanne specializes in western hospitality, even offering to board guests' horses. The bed and breakfast is within a two-hour drive of Jackson Hole and the Grand Teton and Yellowstone National Parks. Learn more on the Web, www.cruising-america.com/windowonwinds

Window on the Winds Bed & Breakfast

10151 Highway 191, P.O. Box 996
Pinedale, WY 82941
307-367-2600
Fax 307-367-2395
Toll-free 888-367-1345

Candy Cane Cookies

*"These Christmas cookies add a nice variety to the look of your platter of holiday treats,"
said Innkeeper Leanne McClain. She's been making them every year for many years.
Makes approximately 2 dozen cookies.*

1 cup margarine
1 cup powdered sugar
1 egg
1½ teaspoons almond extract
1 teaspoon vanilla extract
2½ cups sifted flour
1 teaspoon salt
red and green food coloring

Candy Glaze

1 egg white
½ teaspoon water
¼ cup crushed peppermint candy
¼ cup sugar

- Preheat oven to 375 degrees.
- With an electric mixer, cream the margarine, powdered sugar, egg, almond extract, and vanilla.
- Beat in the salt and flour, mixing until smooth.
- Divide the dough in half. Tint one half with red food coloring. Tint the other half with green food coloring (or leave natural).
- Cover and refrigerate the dough until it's stiff enough to handle, at least 30 minutes.
- Pinch off small pieces of dough and roll into pencil-shaped strips about 4 inches long.
- Twist a red and green strip together. Bend one end into a candy cane shape and place on a cookie sheet. Continue with rest of dough.
- Bake for approximately 10 minutes or until lightly browned.
- To make the topping, mix together the egg white and water.
- In another bowl, mix the candy and the sugar.
- While cookies are still warm, brush tops with egg mixture and sprinkle with crushed candy. Let cool.

Old Iron Inn Bed & Breakfast

*T*he Old Iron Inn is located in Aroostook County, in northern Maine, far from the touristed areas along the coast. This area is so unusual that it is simply known as "The County" throughout Maine and much of the rest of New England, explain innkeepers Kate and Kevin McCartney. Visitors will find that "The County" has the largest geographic area but lowest population density in the Eastern United States and is home to several active Swedish communities. Half the population speaks French.

Kate and Kevin opened the inn in 1992, partly because there were few bed and breakfast inns in this scenic area and partly because they enjoy meeting a wide variety of travelers. As part of her studies as an undergraduate, Kate spent a semester in England and traveled around Europe, staying at B&Bs. She enjoyed the experience and has based the Old Iron Inn on the European model, accommodating guests' assorted comfort and dietary needs.

The name of the inn comes from the McCartney's collection of antique irons that decorates the house. They've found irons hold considerable diversity despite their use as an ordinary household appliance. The McCartneys are avid readers, and their specialized libraries include mysteries, books about Abraham Lincoln, and aviation history. The reading room, open to guests, also boasts forty magazine subscriptions. A monthly music night is also open to guests.

The inn is a turn-of-the-century Arts and Crafts style house, with the original interior oak woodwork intact. The McCartneys have made sensitive renovations, striving to maintain its historical integrity. The four guestrooms are each furnished in oak with highback beds. "There is no television on the premises," said Kate. "There are simply too many other things to do."

The Old Iron Inn Bed & Breakfast

155 High Street
Caribou, ME 04736
207-492-4766

Caramel Walnut Bars

"This is a mouthwatering, delicious bar cookie, especially if you like nuts," said Inn-keeper Kate McCartney. "A tender shortbread crust is topped with nut-filled meringue, all baked to a golden perfection. They are something a little different and are very elegant." Her husband, as well as guests, loves these. Makes 16 bars.

> 1 ½ cups flour
> 1 teaspoon baking powder
> ½ cup butter, softened
> 1 cup sugar
> 2 egg yolks
> 2 tablespoons milk or heavy cream
> 1 teaspoon vanilla extract

Meringue
> 2 egg whites
> 1 cup light brown sugar, packed
> 1 cup coarsely chopped walnuts

■ Preheat oven to 350 degrees. Lightly grease a 9 x 9-inch baking pan.

■ In a medium bowl, sift together the flour and baking powder.

■ Using an electric mixer, cream the butter, sugar, and egg yolks until light and fluffy. At low speed, beat in the flour mixture, then the milk and vanilla extract, just until combined.

■ Turn mixture into pan, spreading evenly.

■ Bake for 20 minutes or until evenly golden brown.

■ For the meringue, beat the egg whites just until stiff. Gradually beat in the brown sugar; stir in nuts. Spread evenly on top of warm crust.

■ Bake for an 20 additional minutes, or until puffed and lightly browned.

■ Cut into bars while still warm. Let cool completely in pan on wire rack.

Birch Tree Inn Bed & Breakfast

*T*he Birch Tree Inn is perhaps best described as a Midwestern farmhouse in the heart of Flagstaff. Built by a contractor from Chicago in 1917, the two-story house has a large side-wrapped porch supported by Corinthian columns.

The home was owned by Joseph Waldhaus for 40 years, beginning in the late 1920s. Joe was a prominent member of the Flagstaff community, having served as a city council member, mayor and postmaster. Following his death in 1969, 22 members of the Sigma Tau Gamma Fraternity called 824 W. Birch their home for three years. In 1972, Sigma Chi took over residence with seven fraternity brothers. Thereafter, the house fell into some disrepair and went through a series of owners.

In 1988, it was the good fortune of Donna and Rodger Pettinger and Sandy and Ed Znetko, lifelong friends from Southern California, to purchase and refurbish the charming home and turn it into the Birch Tree Inn. The innkeepers have five guestrooms, each decorated in a different theme, using family heirlooms, momentoes and hand-made furniture. Downstairs, the living room is a good place to chat with other guests, who may be from any place in the world; the innkeepers have hosted guests from 35 different countries and 49 states. Guests might challenge each other to a game of ppool in the game room or tinkle the ivories on the piano, perhaps for an impromptu singalong.

Flagstaff is most well-known as the largest city closest to the south rim of the Grand Canyon. Visitors also find plenty of hiking, biking, antiquing, other shopping, and other in the area, including visiting Indian ruins or star gazing at the Lowell Observatory. Learn more on the Web, www.birchtreeinn.com

Birch Tree Inn Bed & Breakfast
824 W. Birch Avenue
Flagstaff, AZ 86001
Toll-free 888-774-1042
Fax 520-774-8462

Cashew Drop Cookies

Innkeeper Sandy Znetko created this recipe by trial-and-error, "creating with cashews until I liked the results, which won first place at the County Fair." Makes approximately 5 dozen 2-inch cookies.

1 cup butter, softened
1 cup sugar
1 cup brown sugar, packed
1 egg
$\frac{1}{2}$ cup sour cream
1 teaspoon vanilla extract
3 cups flour
1 teaspoon baking soda
$\frac{1}{2}$ teaspoon salt
$1\frac{1}{2}$ cups salted cashew pieces

Frosting

$\frac{1}{2}$ cup butter
3 tablespoons sour cream
2 cups powdered sugar
$\frac{1}{2}$ teaspoon vanilla extract

- Preheat oven to 350 degrees. Grease cookie sheets.
- With an electric mixer, cream butter, sugar, and brown sugar. Add egg, sour cream, and vanilla.
- In a separate bowl, combine flour, baking soda, and salt. Beat into creamed mixture, blending thoroughly.
- Stir in cashew pieces by hand.
- Drop dough by spoonfuls onto cookie sheets.
- Bake for 12 to 15 minutes, or until lightly browned.
- To make the frosting, mix together the butter, sour cream, powdered sugar, and vanilla. Spread on cooled cookies.

Salisbury House

*W*hether traveling for business or pleasure, from acrss the ocean or just another part of town, guests at Salisbury House are sure to get a true taste of Pacific Northwest hospitality. Innkeeper Cathryn Wiese and her mother, Mary, enjoy the "breakfast" part of their Seattle B&B, using local produce in recipes whenever possible. They may pick berries at the region's berry farms or enjoy pears and apples from their own trees. Cathryn and her husband gather wild huckleberries and wild mushrooms from the local woods and these may end up in pancakes or frittata.

Breakfast is served in the sunny dining room of this large, airy inn. The public rooms have maple floors and fireplaces. Upstairs are four guestrooms, each individually decorated, with crisp white linens and comfy queen beds. A new suite on the lower level has a private entrance with a sitting room, fireplace, refrigerator and large whirlpool tub.

Mary and Cathryn opened their B&B in 1985 and have renovated this fine old mansion, keeping its charm, while adding modern comforts. The inn is on a tree-lined street in the beautiful Capitol Hill neighborhood, within walking distance to shops, restaurants and Volunteer Park, home to the Seattle Asian Art Museum. Guests take advantage of Seattle's excellent public transportation and hop a bus a block away to get to the University of Washington or to explore downtown Seattle's Pike Place Market, piers and Aquarium, historic district and other attractions. Learn more on the Web, www.salisburyhouse.com

Salisbury House

750 16th Avenue East
Seattle, WA 98112
206-328-8682
Fax 206-720-1019

Cathy's Cream Cheese Sugar Cookies

While in college, Cathryn Wiese worked at a kitchen supply store, where a co-worker shared this recipe. She has made a few changes in the 15 years since. "They are a little more difficult to roll out than the standard sugar cookie dough, but they're much tastier," she notes. She uses Mexican vanilla, whenever possible. Makes about 80 cookies, depending on size of cookie cutters.

> 2 cups butter, at room temperature
> 2 cups sugar
> 6 ounces cream cheese, at room temperature
> 2 egg yolks (reserve 1 white for the frosting)
> 1 teaspoon salt
> 2 teaspoons vanilla extract
> 2 teaspoons almond extract
> 5 cups flour

Frosting
> 1 egg white
> 1 cup powdered sugar
> food coloring

- With an electric mixer, cream the butter, sugar, and cream cheese.
- In a small bowl, beat the egg yolks slightly. Beat them into the butter mixture. Add the salt, vanilla, and almond extract, and mix well. Mix in the flour, 1 cup at a time. "The heavy dough may need to be blended by hand."
- Wrap the dough in plastic and refrigerate for about 30 minutes.
- Preheat oven to 350 degrees.
- On a lightly floured surface, roll out the dough until about ¼ inch thick and cut out with cookie cutters.
- Bake the cookies on a heavy, ungreased cookie sheet for 8 to 10 minutes, depending on the thickness of the cookies. "They should be *very* lightly browned when done." Remove to sheets of waxed paper.
- In the meantime, mix the egg white, powdered sugar, and food coloring together to make the frosting. Decorate the cookies when cooled completely. (Editor's note: If you are concerned about salmonella when using raw egg white, make sure you buy pasteurized eggs at the supermarket.)

Watch Hill Bed & Breakfast

*W*hen guests come to Barbara Lauterbach's B&B, they may come for many reasons — but when they come *back*, "food" is always one that draws them. A gourmet chef, Barbara trained at renowned culinary institutes in Paris, Italy, and England. Her food-related career has included developing cooking schools for a chain of department stores, serving as an instructor at the New England Culinary Institute, and acting as a consultant and spokesperson for food-related businesses. She also has done regular television cooking segments and presents classes around the country. When she bought the B&B in 1989, her background was just one of the talents that made innkeeping attractive to her. Guests love to sit and chat during an excellent breakfast, and Barbara holds cooking classes at the B&B.

Watch Hill is one of the oldest homes in Center Harbor. Built circa 1772 by the brother of the town's founder, it has views of Lake Winnipesaukee, just down the street. Guests in the four guestrooms especially enjoy the home's porch in the summer or warming up with a mug of hot cider after skiing or snowmobiling in the winter. Barbara's full country breakfast often showcases New Hampshire products and may feature fresh, hot breads, sausage, bacon, home-fries, fresh fruit, and brown eggs. Guests enjoy the food and the conversation, which often turns to the how her B&B was named (after the champion bull mastiffs Barbara used to raise from the Watch Hill kennel in Cincinnati, Ohio). Watch Hill is a five-minute walk from one of the country's foremost quilt shops, and quilters are frequent guests. "Sometimes they come in vans and take over the whole place!" Barbara said. "They have Show and Tell in the evening, inspecting each other's purchases of fabrics and patterns."

Watch Hill Bed & Breakfast
P.O. Box 1605
Center Harbor, NH 03226
603-253-4334
Fax 603-253-8560

Center Harbor Firehouse Brownies

"Firehouse Brownies" are named in honor of Innkeeper Barbara Lauterbach's neighbor. "He was the fire chief. He helped me out on Christmas Eve when my pipes froze. I had a full house, and it was my first Christmas in New Hampshire on my own. He spent hours in my basement with a hair dryer, thawing the frozen pipes — and the temperature was 10 degrees below! At the next supper, I owed him one." Makes 18 to 24 brownies.

　　4　squares unsweetened chocolate (4 ounces)
　　1　cup butter or margarine
　　4　eggs
　　2　cups sugar
　　1　cup flour
　　½　teaspoon salt
　　1　cup chopped pecans or walnuts
　　1　teaspoon vanilla extract

Frosting
　　2　tablespoons butter or margarine, softened
　1¼　cups powdered sugar, sifted
　　3　tablespoons light cream

Decorative Drizzle Icing
　　2　squares semi-sweet chocolate (2 ounces)
　　1　tablespoon butter or margarine

■ Preheat oven to 325 degrees. Butter a 9 x 13-inch pan.
■ Melt together the unsweetened chocolate and butter or margarine.
■ In a separate bowl, beat the eggs and sugar together.
■ In another bowl, combine the flour, salt, nuts, and vanilla.
■ Beat the melted chocolate-butter mixture and the egg-sugar mixture into the flour mixture. Spread batter in baking pan. Bake for 35 minutes.
■ While the brownies are baking, make the frosting and the icing. For the frosting, beat the butter; add the sugar and beat well. Add the cream and mix until smooth. (Barbara adds, "It will not look like much, but it'll be enough.")
■ To make the decorative drizzle icing, melt together the chocolate and butter in a small pan.
■ When brownies are done baking, cool on a wire rack. Spread frosting over the top of the cooled brownies. With a wire whisk or fork, drizzle the icing over the top of the frosting in quick circles or up, down, and across.

The Graham Bed & Breakfast Inn and Adobe Village

*S*edona, set among the beautiful red rocks that have become popular with travelers everywhere, was discovered by Carol and Roger Redenbaugh in 1992. When they stumbled upon The Graham Inn there, they knew they were "home." Having never stayed in a B&B, they instinctinvely knew that they wanted to be innkeepers. They wrote a business plan on the airplane back to Virginia, found it worked, and flew back the next weekend to finalize the sale. That caused their friends to say, "You're doing WHAT? WHERE?"

The Inn, first in Arizona to be built as a B&B, has six guestrooms, each with private balconies with red rock views, whirlpool tubs and fireplaces and other amenities. In 1997, the Redenbaughs added Adobe Village next door to the main inn, with four luxurious Santa Fe adobe-style cottages centered around a landscaped courtyard. Features include waterfall showers, bath fireplaces, one-of-a-kind furnishings and bread makers. Each casita is of totally different southwest architectural design and decor.

All of the guests enjoy the outdoor pool, hot tub, bicycles, and CD and video collection. Carol and Roger's guests gather before dinner for hors d'oeuvres and conversation, and can sneak homemade cookies from the cookie jar before bed.

The Redenbaughs provide an area map and make suggestions for everything from hiking to vortexes in the red rocks to art galleries and restaurants. Horseback riding, jeep tours, exploring Indian ruins, visiting Slide Rock State Park and shopping are among the favorite activities of guests. Learn more on the Web, www.sedonasfinest.com

The Graham Bed & Breakfast Inn and Adobe Village

150 Canyon Circle Drive
Sedona, AZ 86351
Toll-free 800-228-1425
Fax 520-284-0767

Chocolate Chip Oatmeal Cookies

This recipe is one that has been in the family recipe books for years, said Carol Redenbaugh. But despite its age, its popularity is still quite intact. Guests help themselves to cookies such as this every night from the cookie jar in the first-floor gathering room. They can enjoy a cookie or two after a soak in the hot tub under the stars. Makes about 40 cookies.

    1 cup butter-flavored shortening
    ¾ cup sugar
    ¾ cup dark brown sugar, packed
    2 eggs
    1 teaspoon vanilla extract
 1½ cups flour
    1 teaspoon baking soda
    1 teaspoon salt, optional
    2 cups old-fashioned or quick-cooking rolled oats
    1 12-ounce bag semi-sweet chocolate chips

- Preheat oven to 375 degrees. Grease cookie sheets.
- With an electric mixer, beat shortening and sugars. Then beat in eggs and vanilla.
- In a separate bowl, stir together flour, baking soda and optional salt. Then beat into egg mixture.
- Stir in oats and chips by hand.
- Drop golf ball-sized balls of dough onto cookie sheets, well-apart from each other.
- Bake for 12 minutes or until golden brown. Remove pans from oven and cool for 5 minutes before removing cookies from pans (if you can wait that long!).

Thorwood and Rosewood Inns

*T*he year was 1983, and in Minnesota, hardly anyone had heard of B&Bs, let alone stayed in one. That was the year that Pam and Dick Thorsen opened two guestrooms in their 1880 home. They had bought the apartment building for their home and to generate a little extra income. But it turned out the Thorsens were perfect for the B&B business: Dick is quite capable of undertaking major historic restoration projects and Pam, the consummate romantic, decorates luxurious suites and entices guests to them. Today they own and operate two historic inns with a total of 15 guestrooms, and the popular inns are often named Minnesota's best and most-romantic getaways. Thorwood, as it is now named, was built as a lumber baron's home in this Mississippi rivertown. Eventually, it was turned into a private hospital and then an apartment house. After unending work, it now has seven guestrooms on three floors, all with fireplaces and/or whirlpools. In 1986, they purchased another historic home that once served as a hospital. Rosewood, owned by the city and in disrepair, was "gutted" to the studs and rebuilt with eight luxurious suites and a gift shop on the back porch. Guests can sequester themselves in luxury, ordering hat box suppers on the weekends, or breakfast served in their suites or in formal dining spaces. Or they can stroll downtown for dinner and coffee. Located only a half-hour from St. Paul, Hastings has a winery, nature center, antique stores, two coffee shops, a toy store, a Scandinavian shop, and a well-loved restaurant, all in town or nearby.

Pam, who is active in historic preservation efforts in the city, creates several special packages and theme weekends. Learn more on the Web, www.thorwoodinn.com

Thorwood and Rosewood Inns

315 Pine Street
Hastings, MN 55033
651-437-3297 ■ Fax 651-437-4129

Chocolate Chip Shortbread

"These are very popular, especially with our three-course picnic teas," said Innkeeper Pam Thorsen. Guests receive a picnic basket, stocked with tea sandwiches, scones and a trio of desserts "that are really yummy but not gooey," and they enjoy their picnic tea in one of Hastings many beautiful parks. The shortbread is also easy to make, delicious and is egg-free. Makes 16 wedges.

$\frac{1}{2}$ cup butter, softened
$\frac{1}{2}$ cup sugar
1 teaspoon vanilla extract
2 cups flour
$\frac{1}{4}$ teaspoon salt
$\frac{1}{2}$ cup mini semi-sweet chocolate chips

- Preheat oven to 375 degrees.
- With an electric mixer on medium speed, beat butter and sugar until light and fluffy.
- Beat in vanilla. Add flour and salt and beat at low speed.
- Stir in chocolate chips by hand.
- Divide dough in half. Press each half into an ungreased 8-inch round cake pan.
- Bake for 12 minutes.
- Score shortbread with a sharp knife, taking care not to cut completely through. When shortbread is cool, break into wedges.

Inn on the Rio

*L*ocated on the Rio Fernando at the base of the Sangre de Cristo Mountains, just east from historic downtown Taos Plaza, the Inn on the Rio has recently been re-born. Innkeepers Robert and Julie Chahalane left the corporate "rat race" back in New England and took on the monumental task of bringing a former landmark back into its glory. Julie, with a master's degree in nutrition, knew she could satisfy her guests' hunger for healthy Southwest treats. Robert, a retired marketing executive with an background in finance and economics, knew he could make the numbers work. But what about the declining physical structures? New friends and neighbors, happy to see the interest of the new innkeepers, offered their knowledge, and the task began.

One renovation highlight is an outdoor, in-ground hot tub that offers a spectacular view of Taos Mountain during the day and the star-studded sky at night. Rooms are decorated in "cowboy casual" and "pueblo picturesque" with blankets, rugs, and art collected from all over New Mexico. Julie's new flowerbeds are filled with hollyhocks, Mexican Hats, and other native plants. The "icing on the cake" has been visits by two Southwest artists who spent several weeks painting murals on the exterior walls, arches over the doorways, and, with painstaking detail, the interiors, including each bathroom! In front of the historic Carmen Valarde Kiva fireplace in the inn's cozy gathering room, Julie offers guests suggestions for dining, sightseeing, and shopping. Robert, an outdoor enthusiast, reveals the best-kept secrets of the great outdoors for close-by hiking, mountain biking, and challenging skiing. Learn more on the Web, www.innontherio.com

Inn on the Rio

Box 6529-NDCBU
910 East Kit Carson Road
Taos, NM 87571
505-758-7199 ■ Fax 505-751-1816
Toll-free 800-859-6752

Chocolate Clouds

These are light, practically fat-free meringue cookies. "Clouds make excellent use of extra egg whites and are loved for their delicate texture and just the right amount of chocolate," said Innkeeper Julie Cahalane. Makes approximately 4 dozen cookies.

       4 egg whites, room temperature
     1/4 teaspoon cream of tartar
       1 cup sugar
    dash salt
     1/2 teaspoon vanilla extract
       1 package (8-ounces) semi-sweet chocolate chips

- Preheat oven to 325 degrees. Line cookie sheets with parchment baking paper.
- With an electric mixer, beat the eggs whites and cream of tartar until stiff.
- Gradually add the sugar, salt, and vanilla extract. Fold in the chocolate chips.
- Drop dough by tablespoonfuls onto cookie sheet. Bake for 20 minutes.
- Turn oven off and keep cookies in the oven for another 20 minutes.
- Remove from oven and enjoy. Store remaining cookies in an air tight container.

The Doanleigh Inn

*T*he Doanleigh Inn, Kansas City's first B&B, was named after one of the original innkeeper's great-great-great grandmothers, Sarah Doanleigh of Wales. The current innkeepers, Cynthia Brogdon and Terry Maturo, purchased the grand inn in 1985 and have begun extensive renovations of the 1907 Georgian mansion, once a majestic private home.

The couple's interest in innkeeping began after Cynthia spent several years traveling throughout the country on business. Tiring of hotels and seeking more personalized service in a relaxed atmosphere, she began staying in B&Bs and country inns. Today, as innkeepers, Cynthia and Terry try to offer the service and pampering for their business and leisure guests that they would appreciate themselves. Computer modem access in guestrooms, early breakfasts, in-room speaker phones, and other conveniences are all efforts to meet the needs of business travelers. And, while the breakfast may be served as early as 6:00 in the morning, it is still delicious gourmet fare that has earned Cynthia quite a reputation. Guests enjoy evening hors d'oeuvres and wine, as well.

In the heart of Kansas City, the Doanleigh Inn overlooks historic Hyde Park, just 12 minutes from downtown. It is closer still to the famed Country Club Plaza, Hallmark Crown Center, and the University of Missouri, and it is near the Nelson-Atkins Museum of Art and other attractions. Learn more on the Web, www.doanleigh.com

The Doanleigh Inn

217 East 37th Street
Kansas City, MO 64111
816-753-2667
Fax 816-531-5185

Chocolate Decadence Cookies

"This is an outstanding cookie that always gets rave reviews!" Innkeeper Cynthia Brogdon notes that it's necessary to make this many cookies because they disappear so quickly. But if the amount seems daunting, you can halve the recipe or freeze batter dropped onto a cookie sheet until firm, then remove and place in freezer bags (increase baking time of frozen dough to 15 minutes). Makes 72 large or 100 small cookies.

2 cups semi-sweet chocolate chips
6 ounces unsweetened chocolate
1 ½ cups butter
⅔ cup flour
½ teaspoon baking powder
½ teaspoon salt
6 eggs
2 cups sugar
4 teaspoons vanilla extract
3 cups semi-sweet chocolate chips
2 cups chopped pecans
2 cups chopped walnuts

- Preheat oven to 350 degrees. Lightly grease cookie sheets.
- In a microwave, melt together 2 cups semi-sweet chips, unsweetened chocolate, and butter. Stir until smooth.
- In a separate bowl, sift together the flour, baking powder, and salt.
- With an electric mixer, beat the eggs, sugar, and vanilla until fluffy.
- Beat the chocolate mixture into the egg mixture. Then beat in the flour mixture. Note: dough will be thin.
- Finally, stir in the chocolate chips and nuts by hand.
- Drop dough by tablespoonfuls onto cookie sheet. Bake for 10 to 12 minutes.

Rose Manor Bed & Breakfast

*W*estern Lancaster County is a region of picturesque rolling farmland dotted with quaint villages. Rose Manor rests in a quiet residential neighborhood in the borough of Manheim, far from tour buses and crowds. Rose Manor was built in 1905 by a local lumbermill owner and still contains its original chestnut woodwork and cabinetry. The decor is elegant and old-fashioned, somewhat Victorian, with comfortable chairs and sofas and antiques. An herbal theme is reflected in the names of the guestrooms, in decorative touches throughout the house, and in the cooking. The extensive herb gardens supply the perfect ingredients to make breakfast memorable. Tea is also served in the cozy tea room, by prior reservation.

When they began innkeeping in 1995, Susan Jenal and her mother, Anne, combined their love of cooking, pretty things, gardening, meeting new people, and hard work. Native New Yorkers, they've come to know the area better than some locals, yet they still see Lancaster through visitors' eyes and provide guests with a variety of suggestions on how to best enjoy their stay.

Area attractions and activities include Amish farms, the Pennsylvania Renaissance Faire, outlet shopping, Hershey, farmers markets, antiquing, the Strasburg Railroad, local historic sites and museums, bicycling, fishing and quilting. Rose Manor is also a convenient starting point for day trips to Gettysburg and Longwood Gardens.

Rose Manor Bed & Breakfast
124 South Linden Street
Manheim, PA 17545
717-664-4932
Fax 717-664-1611

Chocolate-Dipped Oatmeal Shortbread

This shortbread is perfect with tea and is served at afternoon teas, held at Rose Manor by reservation. "This recipe came from a friend who doesn't like chocolate, but loves these," said Innkeeper Susan Jenal. Makes 3 dozen cookies.

>1 cup margarine, softened
>1 1/4 cups flour
>1/2 teaspoon salt
>1 cup powdered sugar
>2 teaspoons vanilla extract
>2 cups old-fashioned rolled oats
>1 cup semi-sweet chocolate chips

- With an electric mixer, cream the margarine. Add the flour and salt and stir well.
- Beat in the powdered sugar and vanilla.
- Stir in the oats, by hand, if necessary, and mix well.
- Shape the dough into two logs and roll into plastic wrap. Chill overnight.
- When ready to bake, preheat oven to 350 degrees.
- Cut logs into 1/4-inch slices. Bake on an ungreased cookie sheet 12 to 15 minutes.
- Remove cookies to a rack and cool.
- Melt chocolate chips in a small bowl in the microwave.
- Dip one half of each cookie in the melted chocolate.
- Lay dipped cookies on plastic wrap-covered cookie sheet and refrigerate until set. Store in a tightly-covered container.

The Inn on the Green

*T*his landmark Southern Colonial home rests atop the hill overlooking the MaCalGrove Country Club. Each of the four guestrooms here is named after a Southern city and features garden decor, inspired by the gardens surrounding the inn and inviting summer guests to relax and enjoy the birds and butterflies.

The Jilek family — Brad and Shelley and their kids, Patrick and Kristina, along with miniature schnauzer Winston — welcome guests who come to stroll through the gardens, answer the challenge of the golf course, or identify the many birds that call the estate home. After a day biking on the Root River Trail, flyfishing the many trout streams or antiquing, or cross-country skiing, guests can relax in the poolroom and use the whirlpool or sauna.

Brad, an electrical contractor, will answer those building and remodeling questions. But to really get him talking, mention his Harley-Davidson or Z-3 Roadster. He has mapped out some of the greateest backroads in Minnesota's Bluff Country and will not only share his route, but will share his garage with guests driving special bikes and cars. Shelley, a former teacher, loves cooking and creative forms of sewing and needlework. She is happy to share recipes and has been featured in several cookbooks that are for sale at the Inn. Her evening desserts, which she serves in each guestroom, are legendary in Bluff Country. All the guestrooms have her handmade quilts, and guests awaken to the aroma of a gourmet breakfast. Learn more on the Web, www.bluffcountry.com/inngreen.htm

The Inn on the Green

Route 1, Box 205
Caledonia, MN 55921
507-724-2818
Fax 507-724-5571
Toll-free 800-445-9523

Chocolate Drop Cookies

Innkeeper Shelley Jilek grew up on a small dairy farm, and this recipe was her mother's favorite way to use sour milk. Shelley has reworked this family favorite recipe using buttermilk. She also serves the cookies as a special holiday treat, decorated with red and green cherries. Makes 24 cookies.

½ cup butter
1 cup sugar
1 egg
2 squares unsweetened chocolate, melted
2 cups flour
½ teaspoon salt
½ teaspoon baking soda
¾ cup buttermilk
¾ cup chopped nuts, optional
  chocolate frosting
  nuts or cherries for garnish

- Preheat oven to 400 degrees. Liberally grease a cookie sheet.
- With an electric mixer, cream the butter and sugar. Beat in the egg and melted chocolate.
- In a separate bowl, mix together the flour, salt and baking soda. Alternately add the flour mixture and the buttermilk to the butter mixture. Add the nuts, if desired.
- Drop rounded tablespoonfuls of dough on cookie sheet. Bake for 12 minutes.
- Cool on a rack. Frost with your favorite chocolate frosting and garnish with a nut or cherry.

Watch Hill Bed & Breakfast

*W*hen guests come to Barbara Lauterbach's B&B, they may come for many reasons — but when they come *back*, "food" is always one that draws them. A gourmet chef, Barbara trained at renowned culinary institutes in Paris, Italy, and England. Her food-related career has included developing cooking schools for a chain of department stores, serving as an instructor at the New England Culinary Institute, and acting as a consultant and spokesperson for food-related businesses. She also has done regular television cooking segments and presents classes around the country. When she bought the B&B in 1989, her background was just one of the talents that made innkeeping attractive to her. Guests love to sit and chat during an excellent breakfast, and Barbara holds cooking classes at the B&B.

Watch Hill is one of the oldest homes in Center Harbor. Built circa 1772 by the brother of the town's founder, it has views of Lake Winnipesaukee, just down the street. Guests in the four guestrooms especially enjoy the home's porch in the summer or warming up with a mug of hot cider after skiing or snowmobiling in the winter. Barbara's full country breakfast often showcases New Hampshire products and may feature fresh, hot breads, sausage, bacon, home-fries, fresh fruit, and brown eggs. Guests enjoy the food and the conversation, which often turns to the how her B&B was named (after the champion bull mastiffs Barbara used to raise from the Watch Hill kennel in Cincinnati, Ohio). Watch Hill is a five-minute walk from one of the country's foremost quilt shops, and quilters are frequent guests. "Sometimes they come in vans and take over the whole place!" Barbara said. "They have Show and Tell in the evening, inspecting each other's purchases of fabrics and patterns."

Watch Hill Bed & Breakfast
P.O. Box 1605
Center Harbor, NH 03226
603-253-4334
Fax 603-253-8560

Chocolate Madeleines

"This is a tasty variation of the Madeleine, the shell-shaped cookie immortalized by Proust," explained Barbara Lauterbach, innkeeper. "I think he would have remembered these very well!" She uses shell molds that come 8 or 12 to a pan, found in most cookware shops. She also notes these freeze nicely. Makes approximately 24 cookies.

½ cup plus 2 tablespoons butter
3 ounces semi-sweet chocolate
2 tablespoons unsweetened cocoa
¾ cup sugar
1¼ cups flour, sifted
pinch salt
3 eggs
2 egg yolks
1 teaspoon vanilla extract

Frosting

2 ounces bittersweet or unsweetened chocolate
1 tablespoon butter

- Preheat oven to 350 degrees. Lightly butter the molds.
- In a saucepan over low heat, melt the butter and chocolate, stirring until chocolate is melted.
- In another saucepan, combine cocoa, sugar, flour, and salt.
- In a bowl, lightly beat eggs, yolks, and vanilla until well blended.
- Stir chocolate mixture into dry cocoa mixture. Add egg mixture and blend well.
- Place saucepan over very low heat. Stirring constantly, let mixture warm for approximately 2 minutes. (It must not turn truly hot. Test with finger.) Remove from heat.
- Fill molds half full with batter, being careful to not overfill.
- Bake for 12 minutes. Cool on rack.
- For frosting, melt bittersweet chocolate with butter in a saucepan.
- Place waxed paper under a cookie rack. Paint Madeleines with melted chocolate mixture while on rack.

The Inn at Maplewood Farm

*L*aura and Jayme Simoes left busy lives working in a metropolitan public relations firm for life literally along a slow lane. They purchased this bucolic, picture-perfect New England farmhouse and entered careers as innkeepers. Their inn, which has welcomed visitors for two hundred years, sits on 14 acres along a winding country road, just a short drive from the town of Hillsborough. Guests looking for a quiet getaway are delighted to find that the nearest neighbors are a few cows and the 1,400-acre Fox State Forest.

Breakfast is made from locally grown and produced foods and delivered by basket to the guestrooms for a "breakfast in bed" experience. While enjoying the fireplace or rocking on the porch are the chosen daytime pursuits of many guests, there is plenty to do in the area. Laura and Jayme love directing guests to little-known antique stores, historic villages, picnic spots, and waterfalls, all within a few minutes' drive.

The Inn's four guestrooms are decorated in antiques, including an antique radio at bedside in each. Jayme's infatuation with the Golden Age of Radio has led to his own transmitter on the farm, from which he broadcasts old-time radio programs to the guestrooms via the vintage radios. Request a favorite and, chances are, he's got it in this 1,000-plus show collection. Learn more on the Web, www.conknet.com/maplewoodfarm/

The Inn at Maplewood Farm

P.O. Box 1478
447 Center Road
Hillsborough, NH 03224
603-464-4242
Fax 603-464-5401
Toll-free 800-644-6695

Chocolate Pecan Butterscotch Shortbread

"This is a very easy recipe for chewy, buttery shortbread that our guests devour," said Innkeeper Laura Simoes. "Because the dough is thick, I use a heavy-duty stand mixer to stir in everything, down to the pecans." Guests might find these cookies on a plate on the nightstand prior to bedtime. Makes 18 cookies.

    1 teaspoon vanilla extract
    1 cup butter
    1 cup dark brown sugar, packed
    2 cups flour
    1 cup semi-sweet chocolate chips (or 1 cup toffee pieces for a non-chocolate variation)
    1 cup chopped pecans

- Preheat oven to 350 degrees. Grease a 9 x 13-inch pan.
- With an electric mixer, cream the vanilla, butter, and brown sugar.
- Add the flour, chocolate chips, and pecans.
- Press dough into pan in until the dough is no more than $\frac{1}{2}$-inch thick. Bake for 10 minutes, turn pan, and bake for another 10 minutes.
- Cut into squares while still warm. Cool before serving.

The Doanleigh Inn

*T*he Doanleigh Inn, Kansas City's first B&B, was named after one of the original innkeeper's great-great-great grandmothers, Sarah Doanleigh of Wales. The current innkeepers, Cynthia Brogdon and Terry Maturo, purchased the grand inn in 1985 and have begun extensive renovations of the 1907 Georgian mansion, once a majestic private home.

The couple's interest in innkeeping began after Cynthia spent several years traveling throughout the country on business. Tiring of hotels and seeking more personalized service in a relaxed atmosphere, she began staying in B&Bs and country inns. Today, as innkeepers, Cynthia and Terry try to offer the service and pampering for their business and leisure guests that they would appreciate themselves. Computer modem access in guestrooms, early breakfasts, in-room speaker phones, and other conveniences are all efforts to meet the needs of business travelers. And, while the breakfast may be served as early as 6:00 in the morning, it is still delicious gourmet fare that has earned Cynthia quite a reputation. Guests enjoy evening hors d'oeuvres and wine, as well.

In the heart of Kansas City, the Doanleigh Inn overlooks historic Hyde Park, just 12 minutes from downtown. It is closer still to the famed Country Club Plaza, Hallmark Crown Center, and the University of Missouri, and it is near the Nelson-Atkins Museum of Art and other attractions. Learn more on the Web, www.doanleigh.com

The Doanleigh Inn
217 East 37th Street
Kansas City, MO 64111
816-753-2667
Fax 816-531-5185

Chocolate Raspberry Streusel Squares

"These rich squares combine the best of raspberry and chocolate. Then, to top it off, we've added a streusel topping!" Innkeeper Cynthia Brogdon says she often cuts the squares into bite-sized morsels for easier snacking. Makes 18 bars.

1½ cups flour
1½ cups old-fashioned rolled oats
½ cup sugar
½ cup brown sugar, packed
1 teaspoon baking powder
¼ teaspoon salt
1 cup margarine or butter, chilled
1 cup seedless raspberry preserves or jam
1 cup semi-sweet chocolate chips
¼ cup chopped walnuts

■ Preheat the oven to 375 degrees. Grease a 9 x 9-inch baking pan.
■ In a large bowl, stir together the flour, oats, sugar, brown sugar, baking powder, and salt.
■ Cut in the margarine with a pastry cutter or fork until the mixture is crumbly. Reserve one cup of the mixture for streusel.
■ Press the remaining oat mixture into the bottom of the pan.
■ Bake for 10 minutes.
■ Spread the preserves over the crust. Sprinkle evenly with the chocolate chips.
■ Combine the reserved oat mixture and the nuts. Sprinkle over the chocolate and pat down gently. Bake for 30 to 35 minutes.
■ Cool completely and cut into bars.

Lamb's Inn Bed & Breakfast

*D*ick and Donna Messerschmidt returned to the Little Willow Valley near Richland Center, Wisconsin, after 32 years away. They bought Donna's parents 180-acre dairy farm and completely restored the house to appear as it did when Albert Misslich brought his bride home in the late 1800s, adding modern conveniences.

The large kitchen, with Donna's grandmother's round oak table, is the center of the Bed & Breakfast, with a formal dining room, living room and library open to guests, as well. Coffee is often enjoyed on the enclosed porch. A new cottage, built in 1990 for Dick and Donna to live in while renovating the farmhouse, has two guest suites.

Breakfast, served in the dining room, is Donna and Dick's favorite part of innkeeping, where the conversation flows, as does hot coffee, for sometimes as long as two hours. Entreés that often appear include blueberry pancakes with an orange sauce, Italian quiche, or stuffed French toast with an apricot sauce. Warm muffins or bread and fresh fruit are always served, as well. In the fall, fresh applesauce and granola might be on the menu.

Guests enjoy feeding the trout in the backyard spring, petting the cats, watching the goats or just going for a quiet walk in the country. In nearby Spring Green, Frank Lloyd Wright's Taliesen and the House on the Rock can be toured, or guests can attend Shakespeare under the stars at American Players Theater. Guests also enjoy visiting Amish farms, canoeing the Kickapoo River or biking the Sparta-Elroy bike trail. Learn more on the Web, www.lambs-inn.com

Lamb's Inn Bed & Breakfast
23761 Misslich Road
Richland Center, WI 53581
608-585-4301

Coconut Oatmeal Cookies

"This is a family favorite," said Innkeeper Donna Messerschmidt, "so I usually double the recipe and freeze the cookies on a cookie sheet." Then she places the frozen dough in a plastic freezer bag and takes out what she needs to bake fresh, warm cookies to welcome guests. Makes 72 cookies.

1 cup butter-flavored shortening
1 cup sugar
1 cup brown sugar, packed
2 eggs
1 teaspoon vanilla extract
2 teaspoons baking soda
1 teaspoon baking powder
1 teaspoon salt
2 cups flour
2 cups quick-cooking or old-fashioned rolled oats
2 cups coconut
2 cups semi-sweet chocolate chips

- With an electric mixer, cream shortening, sugar, and brown sugar.
- Add the eggs, vanilla, baking soda, baking powder, salt, flour, oats, coconut and chocolate chips. Dough will be stiff.
- Chill dough, covered, for several hours or overnight.
- When ready to bake, preheat oven to 300 degrees.
- Roll dough into 1-inch balls or use a 1½-inch ice cream scoop and place on greased cookie sheets.
- Bake for 15 minutes. Cool and enjoy.

Apple Gate Bed & Breakfast

Seasonal fresh fruit is always a part of breakfast at the Apple Gate, and that includes fresh berries from a neighbor's organic farm, as well as apples, of course. Because Apple Gate is located just across the street from a ninety-acre apple orchard, Innkeeper Dianne Legenhausen chose an apple motif to decorate the inn, including naming the four guestrooms after apple varieties. Even Dianne and Ken's one hundred-pound yellow lab, Mac, is named after the Macintosh apple (the cat, Jessie, however, was acquired before the inn and has no apple ties).

Before innkeeping, Dianne taught music to elementary-age children and Ken was a police officer specializing in emergency rescues. While they had many friends in Long Island, New York, where they lived and worked for many years, they decided to head for the Monadnock region of New Hampshire, said to be picture-perfect Currier and Ives country, for their second careers as innkeepers.

They found this 1832 Colonial home just two miles from downtown Peterborough. It offered spacious accommodations for guests, including a double parlor, where guests may enjoy a fire, the library, or a TV and collection of videos. Peterborough is home to the Sharon Arts Center, and the Legenhausen's bed-and-breakfast is just a few miles from the Temple Mountain and Windblown ski areas.

Apple Gate Bed & Breakfast
199 Upland Road
Peterborough, NH 03458
603-924-6543

Crescent Cookies

"When we were kids, my Mom used to bake hundreds of Christmas cookies," with this recipe among them, said Innkeeper Dianne Legenhausen. Her mother was challenged to find securing hiding spots. "We soon discovered her favorite hiding place was the freezer. To this day, I still love frozen cookies!" Dianne lets these thaw before serving them to guests, however! Makes about 42 cookies.

$1\frac{1}{4}$ cups butter, softened
10 tablespoons powdered sugar
2 teaspoons vanilla extract
4 cups flour
2 cups finely chopped pecans or walnuts (not an optional ingredient!)
    powdered sugar

- Preheat oven to 325 degrees. Grease cookie sheets.
- With an electric mixer, cream butter, powdered sugar and vanilla.
- Beat in 1 cup of the flour. Then beat in second cup of flour.
- By hand, stir in remaining 2 cups of flour.
- Stir in the nuts. Dough will be very stiff.
- Shape the dough into logs about the size of a finger, then turn ends into crescent shapes.
- Place crescents on greased cookie sheets.
- Bake for 45 minutes. Remove from oven and cool.
- Roll cookies in powdered sugar.

Yankee Hill Inn Bed & Breakfast

*T*he ambiance of quiet, small town life in the heart of the Kettle Moraine recreational area is what Yankee Hill Inn Bed and Breakfast Innkeepers Peg and Jim Stahlman find draws guests to their two historic homes-turned-B&Bs.

Yankee Hill Inn B&B is comprised of two historic homes restored by the Stahlmans. One is a Sheboygan County landmark, a Queen Anne Victorian–style, built in 1891. The other is an 1870 Gothic Italianate listed on the National Register of Historic Places. Both were built in the "Yankee Hill" area of Plymouth by hard-working, affluent brothers, Henry and Gilbert Huson.

Yankee Hill Inn has 12 guestrooms, decorated with period antiques and other touches to reflect historic lodging. Six guestrooms have single whirlpool tubs. Landscaped yards, parlors, fireplaces, and an enclosed front porch allow the guests to gather and relax. Each morning, guests wake up to the aroma of a full breakfast, featuring home-baked muffins and breads, and the cookie jar is open to guests.

From the Inn, guests take a short walk through Huson Park and across the Mullet River footbridge into downtown Plymouth, where they can explore charming antique and gift shops and dine in excellent restaurants. At the Plymouth Center is an art gallery, the Plymouth Historical Museum, and visitor information.

Outdoor adventures surround Plymouth in the glacially sculpted terrain. Enjoy the Kettle Moraine State Forest, many lakes, marked nature trails and the Ice Age Trail for hiking and biking. The paved Old Plank Road recreational trail, historic Plymouth walking tour, Road America race track and the Kohler Design Center, featuring the latest in Kohler bathroom and kitchen ideas, are also popular. Sheboygan and Lake Michigan are just 15 minutes away. Learn more on the Web, www.yankeehillinn.com

Yankee Hill Inn Bed & Breakfast

405 Collins Street
Plymouth, WI 53073
920-892-2222 ■ Fax 920-892-6228

Crispy Skillet Cookies

"There's no baking, so these are super-easy," noted Innkeeper Peg Stahlman. "They store well, too!" She stores these in a tin, and has made them frequently for holiday treats. Makes approximately 24 cookies.

   2 tablespoons butter or margarine
   2 eggs, beaten
   1 cup sugar
 $\frac{1}{4}$ teaspoon salt
   1 teaspoon vanilla extract
   1 cup chopped dates
   3 cups crispy rice cereal
 $\frac{1}{2}$ cup chopped nuts
     powdered sugar
     coconut

- In a large skillet, melt butter over low heat.
- Stir in eggs, sugar, salt, vanilla and dates. Cook, stirring constantly, until mixture thickens (about 8 minutes).
- Stir in cereal and nuts until mixture is cool enough to be handled.
- Turn out on waxed paper which has been sprinkled with powdered sugar and coconut. Divide and shape into two rolls, rolling outsides in powdered sugar and coconut.
- Chill until firm enough to slice. Then slice at least $\frac{1}{4}$-inch thick and serve.

Thorwood and Rosewood Inns

The year was 1983, and in Minnesota, hardly anyone had heard of B&Bs, let alone stayed in one. That was the year that Pam and Dick Thorsen opened two guestrooms in their 1880 home. They had bought the apartment building for their home and to generate a little extra income. But it turned out the Thorsens were perfect for the B&B business: Dick is quite capable of undertaking major historic restoration projects and Pam, the consummate romantic, decorates luxurious suites and entices guests to them. Today they own and operate two historic inns with a total of 15 guestrooms, and the popular inns are often named Minnesota's best and most-romantic getaways. Thorwood, as it is now named, was built as a lumber baron's home in this Mississippi rivertown. Eventually, it was turned into a private hospital and then an apartment house. After unending work, it now has seven guestrooms on three floors, all with fireplaces and/or whirlpools. In 1986, they purchased another historic home that once served as a hospital. Rosewood, owned by the city and in disrepair, was "gutted" to the studs and rebuilt with eight luxurious suites and a gift shop on the back porch. Guests can sequester themselves in luxury, ordering hat box suppers on the weekends, or breakfast served in their suites or in formal dining spaces. Or they can stroll downtown for dinner and coffee. Located only a half-hour from St. Paul, Hastings has a winery, nature center, antique stores, two coffee shops, a toy store, a Scandinavian shop, and a well-loved restaurant, all in town or nearby.

Pam, who is active in historic preservation efforts in the city, creates several special packages and theme weekends. Learn more on the Web, www.thorwoodinn.com

Thorwood and Rosewood Inns

315 Pine Street
Hastings, MN 55033
651-437-3297 ■ Fax 651-437-4129

Double Almond Journey Cakes

When guests depart Thorwood or Rosewood Inns, they are given a little bag of "journey cakes," along with a story that tells about sharing the cakes and enjoying prosperity thereafter. These rich cookies are made in a diamond-shaped tart pan, and are sometimes served at tea-time here, dolloped with whipped cream. You can serve them as dessert and easily make them in a miniature muffin pan. Makes approximately 3 dozen cookies.

    1 cup butter, softened
    ½ cup sugar
    1 egg
    1 teaspoon almond extract
    2½ cups flour
    ¼ teaspoon salt

Filling

    4 eggs, well-beaten
    3 cups coarsely ground blanched almonds
    1 cup sugar
    ¼ cup milk
    1 teaspoon almond extract

■ With an electric mixer, cream butter, sugar, egg and almond extract.
■ Beat in flour and salt just until all ingredients are blended.
■ Cover and chill dough thoroughly.
■ Pinch off dough and press onto bottoms and sides of miniature tart tins or muffin pans, spreading as thinly and evenly as possible.
■ Preheat oven to 325 degrees.
■ In a large bowl, making filling by stirring together eggs, almonds, sugar, milk and almond extract.
■ Spoon 1 to 1½ teaspoonsfuls of filling into each tart or muffin cup.
■ Place tins on baking sheet. Bake until golden (timing depends on size of tart or muffin cup — check after 8 minutes).
■ Cool at least 5 minutes before removing from tart or muffin cups.

Inn on the Rio

*L*ocated on the Rio Fernando at the base of the Sangre de Cristo Mountains, just east from historic downtown Taos Plaza, the Inn on the Rio has recently been re-born. Innkeepers Robert and Julie Chahalane left the corporate "rat race" back in New England and took on the monumental task of bringing a former landmark back into its glory. Julie, with a master's degree in nutrition, knew she could satisfy her guests' hunger for healthy Southwest treats. Robert, a retired marketing executive with an background in finance and economics, knew he could make the numbers work. But what about the declining physical structures? New friends and neighbors, happy to see the interest of the new innkeepers, offered their knowledge, and the task began.

One renovation highlight is an outdoor, in-ground hot tub that offers a spectacular view of Taos Mountain during the day and the star-studded sky at night. Rooms are decorated in "cowboy casual" and "pueblo picturesque" with blankets, rugs, and art collected from all over New Mexico. Julie's new flowerbeds are filled with hollyhocks, Mexican Hats, and other native plants. The "icing on the cake" has been visits by two Southwest artists who spent several weeks painting murals on the exterior walls, arches over the doorways, and, with painstaking detail, the interiors, including each bathroom! In front of the historic Carmen Valarde Kiva fireplace in the inn's cozy gathering room, Julie offers guests suggestions for dining, sightseeing, and shopping. Robert, an outdoor enthusiast, reveals the best-kept secrets of the great outdoors for close-by hiking, mountain biking, and challenging skiing. Learn more on the Web, www.innontherio.com

Inn on the Rio

Box 6529-NDCBU
910 East Kit Carson Road
Taos, NM 87571
505-758-7199 ■ Fax 505-751-1816
Toll-free 800-859-6752

Favorite Decadence Layer Bars

These bars take minutes to make but disappear in seconds, said Innkeeper Julie Cahalane. They combine all her guests' favorite cookie ingredients, but are made in one pan and couldn't be easier. Makes 18 large bars.

$\frac{1}{2}$ cup butter
 2 cups graham cracker crumbs
 1 cup coconut (one 7-ounce package)
 1 12-ounce package semi-sweet chocolate chips
 2 cups chopped pecans
 1 can (14 ounces) sweetened condensed milk

■ Preheat oven to 350 degrees. While the oven preheats, melt the butter in a 9 x 13-inch pan.
■ One layer at a time, sprinkle the graham cracker crumbs, coconut, chocolate chips, and pecans over the melted butter.
■ Pour sweetened condensed milk over all.
■ Bake for 30 minutes. Cool and cut into squares.

The Delforge Place

*B*etsy Delforge's seven-course breakfasts are renowned in Fredericksburg, and no one leaves the table hungry. She may draw from her collection of family recipes found in her sea captain's trunks or from recipes using regional produce or sausage from the Texas Hill Country (for instance, Gillespie County, the Texas peach capital, grows 20 varieties of peaches). Guests gather in the dining room and the delicious courses just keep coming out of Betsy's kitchen, one after another. The Delforge Place is a family business. Betsy and George, her husband, became innkeepers in Fredericksburg in 1985 after George retired from a long career as an aeronautical engineer and Betsy as a dress designer and food consultant. They updated, redecorated, and opened their inn, the dining room of which was built in 1898 as a one-room "Sunday House." Their son, Peter, joined them in innkeeping in 1994, bringing his talents as a former VP with a New York City advertising agency.

Many family heirlooms are in use at the inn, as are heirloom recipes. In the Map Room, for instance, a seven-foot mural map owned by Betsy's great-grandfather hangs on the wall. In the 1800s, he traveled with Admiral Perry and opened up many harbors of the world to trade.

Originally built by German pioneer Ferdinand Koeppen, the inn served as his "Sunday House" when he needed to go to town to attend church and conduct weekend business. Koeppen built it on a tract of land that was set aside by the German Emigration Company for a community garden, so it was moved to its present site on Ettie Street, just seven blocks from Fredericksburg's popular main street. The Delforges have carefully restored and redecorated each room, including adding a separate suite with a nautical theme that has its own entrance into the inn's courtyard. Outdoor breakfasts are popular in mild weather. Learn more on the Web, www.speakez.net/delforgeplace

The Delforge Place
710 Ettie Street
Fredericksburg, TX 78624
512-997-6212

Fruit Jam Meringue Bars

This recipe originally came from a healthy-eating study done when Betsy Delforge was the president of the Texas Home Economics Association. When Betsy and husband George later opened a bakery, she changed the recipe to this one, notes Pete Delforge, their son. "This is the version which sold so well at the bakery and that we use here at Bed & Breakfast. Since it works well with any fruit jam, we've changed the name accordingly." Makes 42 bars.

      2 cups flour
    ½ teaspoon baking soda
    ½ cup butter
      1 egg
    ½ cup sugar
    ½ teaspoon vanilla extract
    1¼ cups apricot jam (or jam of your choice)

Meringue
      2 egg whites
      2 tablespoons flour
    ½ cup sugar
    ½ cup finely chopped walnuts or nuts of your choice

- Preheat oven to 375 degrees.
- Sift together the flour and baking soda.
- With an electric mixer, cream the butter, egg, sugar, and vanilla. Beat the flour mixture into the creamed mixture.
- With a spatula, press the dough to the edes of an ungreased cookie sheet, making a rectangle approximately 13 x 14 inches in size. Spread the jam evenly over the dough, all the way to the edges.
- Bake for 15 minutes, or until very lightly browned.
- Turn the oven down to 300 degrees while preparing the meringue.
- Beat the egg whites until stiff. Stir in the flour and sugar.
- Spread the meringue over the slightly-cooked jam and sprinkle with walnuts.
- Return bars to the oven and bake for 15 more minutes.

The Gosby House

*T*he Gosby House, an authentic Queen Anne Victorian in Pacific Grove, California, with National Historic Landmark status, was actually the second inn in the Post family's collection of inns call the Four Sisters Inns — a collection that started quite unintentionally.

When Roger and Sally Post moved to Monterey from Los Angeles in the early 1970s, they bought a gorgeous, multi-gabled Victorian home overlooking Monterey Bay. Their intent was simply to raise their four daughters there, but the house, christened "Green Gables" by a previous owner who had opened it to travelers, still attracted the attention of coastal visitors. The Posts received so many inquiries from travelers who wanted to stay in the stately dwelling, with incredible ocean views from nearly every room, they finally opened it to guests in the summer months. The girls simply reshuffled their living quarters every summer.

As it turned out, the Posts were natural innkeepers. In 1978, they opened the Gosby House in nearby Pacific Grove as their first year 'round inn. Today, the family business has become the Four Sisters Inns and employs 350 people, operating some of the finest elegant, intimate hotels in the west. The growing collection of charming inns pampers guests with full country breakfasts, morning newspapers, conceirge service, in-room phones and home-baked cookies. Many rooms have fireplaces and guests may borrow bikes at most inns. The inns are located in downtown San Francisco, Yountville in Napa Valley, Carmel-by-the-Sea, Dana Point, Seattle, and on Whidbey Island, a 20-minute ferry ride across Puget Sound from Seattle. Learn more on the Web, www.foursisters.com

The Gosby House

c/o Four Sisters Inns
P.O. Box 3073
Monterey, CA 93942
Toll-free 800-234-1425 ■ Fax 831-649-4822

Fudge Mound Cookies

Guests at the Gosby House, one of the Four Sisters Inns where the cookie jar is always full, never guess there are mashed potatoes in here. The chocolate and cinnamon are a marvelous combination, and the hint of mocha in the frosting is irresistible. Make sure you don't stack leftovers or they'll stick together. Makes 3 dozen cookies.

1	cup mashed potatoes
¾	cup sugar
¾	cup light brown sugar, packed
½	cup butter-flavored shortening
1	egg
1	teaspoon vanilla extract
2	cups flour
6	tablespoons unsweetened cocoa
2	teaspoons cinnamon
1	teaspoon baking powder
1	teaspoon baking soda
1	teaspoon salt
½	teaspoon nutmeg
½	cup milk

Frosting

2	cups powdered sugar
3 to 4	teaspoons sweet cocoa
½	cup hot coffee, divided
½	teaspoon vanilla extract

- With an electric mixer, cream potatoes, sugar, brown sugar, shortening, egg and vanilla.
- In a separate bowl, stir together the flour, cocoa, cinnamon, baking powder, baking soda, salt and nutmeg. Add the flour mixture to the creamed mixture alternately with the milk.
- Allow dough to stand for 10 minutes while preheating the oven to 350 degrees and greasing cookie sheets. Drop by tablespoons at least 2 inches apart onto cookie sheets. Bake for 12 to 15 minutes, until tops of cookies appear dry. Let cool thoroughly before frosting.
- For the frosting: Whisk or beat together the powdered sugar, cocoa, ¼ cup of the hot coffee and vanilla. Thin to a spreading consistency with more coffee.

The Stone Hearth Inn

*G*uests of The Stone Hearth Inn awaken each day to the natural beauty of Lake Superior, the world's largest freshwater lake. This fully renovated 1920s inn cast its spell on Susan and Charlie Michels. Charlie bought the property in 1989, always having dreamt of living on "big water," and spent a year giving the rundown place a facelift, preserving original details. Susan was a guest the first month he opened; they were married a year later.

The inn's most striking feature might be its veranda, which spans the breadth of the building. Adirondack furniture invites guests to linger here, watching the waves or the calm lake, before retiring to a guestroom in the main building or in the private Boathouse or Carriage House. The Boathouse is literally perched on Superior's shore, and the Carriage House is only 40 feet from the water's edge. Three of the four guestrooms in the main lodge have lake views.

The lakeside dining room's maple hardwood flooring and hand-crafted pine furniture are the perfect backdrop for sunrises and the tantalizing smell of the Michels' unique regional cooking. Menus vary, but Charlie's specialty is blueberry wild rice pancakes; Susan's is delicately spiced French toast stuffed with cream cheese, nuts, and seasonal fruits. Local specialties also make appearances: sausage of trout or duck, northwoods maple syrup, homegrown garden produce, fresh duck eggs.

Twenty kilometers of groomed and tracked cross-country ski trails leave from the inn's front door. Visitors looking for other action spend their days exploring the Superior Hiking Trail, golfing, trout fishing, skiing, or shopping in quaint Grand Marais. An underwater trail for divers is soon to be open. A number of state parks along the "north shore" of Lake Superior offer good hiking and Superior views. Learn more on the Web, www.lakesuperior-northshore.com/stonehearth/

The Stone Hearth Inn
1118 Highway 61 East
Little Marais, MN 55614
218-226-3020 ■ Fax 218-226-3466
Toll-free 888-206-3020

Grandma Catherine's Pinwheel Date Cookies

"When I was 9-years-old, my widowed grandfather married a delightful woman named Catherine," said Innkeeper Susan Michels. "She made great piecrusts, drank full cream in her coffee, taught me how to make French fries from scratch, and always had a full cookie jar!"' Grandma Catherine makes three batches of these at the holidays – one for each side of the family and one to keep." At the Inn, these are a great compliment to the mulled cider we serve in the autumn." They are time-consuming, but simple, and well-worth the effort, she notes. Makes 4 dozen cookies

- 1 cup sugar
- 1 cup brown sugar, packed
- 1 cup butter-flavored shortening
- 3 eggs
- 4 cups flour
- $\frac{1}{2}$ teaspoon salt
- 1 teaspoon baking powder
- 1 teaspoon baking soda
- 1 pound dates, chopped
- $\frac{1}{2}$ cup sugar
- $\frac{1}{2}$ cup water
- 1 teaspoon cinnamon
- 2 tablespoons lemon juice
- 1 cup chopped pecans

■ With an electric mixer, cream the sugar, brown sugar, and shortening. Beat in the eggs, one at a time.

■ In another bowl, sift together the flour, salt, baking powder, and baking soda. Add the flour mixture to the creamed mixture to form a stiff dough.

■ Divide the dough into two portions, wrap in plastic wrap, and chill overnight.

■ After the dough has chilled, cook the dates, sugar, and water in a saucepan until thick. Add the cinnamon, lemon juice, and pecans to the date mixture and let cool.

■ Roll the chilled dough into rectangles. Spread $\frac{1}{2}$ of the date filling over each.

■ Roll each rectangle up, wrap, and chill overnight.

■ The following day, preheat oven to 375 degrees. Slice the rolls into $\frac{1}{4}$-inch cookies and place on a cookie sheet. Bake for 10 minutes.

Thurston House

*T*hurston House was once the winter getaway for wealthy businessman Cyrus B. Thurston of Minneapolis. Built in 1885, Thurston House has been restored to its original splendor. The pine and cyprus woodwork gleams, from a magnificent built-in dining room server and original hardwood floors, to six beautiful mantels and wonderful wood paneling.

After 18 years in the corporate world, Carole Ballard was ready for a change. "Going from a Fortune 500 company to being self-employed was a big change, but one for the better!" she notes. Thurston House was completely renovated and opened for business September 15, 1992. Four cozy guestrooms have lake views, a soaking tub or something special in each room. Carole is on hand to tell guests the history of the home, as well as interesting area history.

Located just five miles north of downtown Orlando on five wooded acres, Thurston House's serene atmosphere belies its convenient location. The grounds include over an acre of fruit trees, flowering bushes, and herb and flower gardens. Guests amble through the camellia bushes, hide away on secluded benches, play croquet, or fish from the banks of tranquil Lake Eulalia. Birdwatching is another favorite activity among visitors. In the evening, guests sip wine and visit on the exquisite wrap-around porch.

Carole greets early risers with the aroma of baked goods and fresh brewed coffee. She serves her delectable breakfast by candlelight in the beautifully restored dining room. Learn more on the Web, www.thurstonhouse.com

Thurston House

851 Lake Avenue
Maitland, FL 32751
407-539-1911
800-843-2721
Fax 407-539-0365

Grandma Webber's Gingersnaps

"Grandma Webber came over from England by herself when she was 17," said Carole Ballard, innkeeper. "She loved to bake so her kitchen always smelled wonderful." Baking these cookies at Thurston House reminds Carole of the aroma of her Grandma's house. Makes 30 cookies.

   ¾ cup butter, softened, or butter-flavored shortening
   1 cup sugar
   ¼ cup molasses
   1 egg, beaten
  2¼ cups flour
   2 teaspoons baking soda
   1 teaspoon cinnamon
   1 teaspoon ground cloves
   1 teaspoon ginger
      sugar for rolling dough

- Preheat oven to 350 degrees. Grease cookie sheets.
- With an electric mixer, cream the butter and sugar. Add the molasses and egg; beat well.
- Add the flour, baking soda, cinnamon, cloves, and ginger, and beat well.
- Roll dough into 1-inch balls, dip in sugar, and press flat 3 inches apart on cookie sheet. "Sprinkle with a couple drops of water for a crinkled effect."
- Bake for 8 to 10 minutes or until tops crinkle and appear set.

Lord Mayor's
Bed & Breakfast Inn

*T*his elegant Edwardian house was the home of the first mayor of Long Beach, Charles H. Windham. His unofficial Edwardian-style title, Lord Mayor, was bestowed by British beauty contestants enjoying the amenities of this seaside resort in the mid-1900s. The Lord Mayor's house was meticulously restored by historians Reuben and Laura Brasser and received the prestigious 1992 Great American Home Award from the National Trust for Historic Preservation for sensitivity in restoration of an historic house.

Their inn has expanded into a collection comprising a total of 12 rooms, with other rooms located in the Cinnamon House, the Apple House and the Garden House. The Garden House was converted from the original horse barn and the others are 1908 city cottages near the original mayor's home.

Located in the heart of Long Beach, Lord Mayor's Inn is close to many major businesses, shopping, dining, and leisure activities. Within walking distance are city and state government offices, the World Trade Center, the Convention Center, Farmers Market, and the Blue Line rapid transit.

Gracious hospitality awaits guests in the Brassers' home. These innkeepers have a reputation for friendliness and fabulous food. Enjoy coffee in the kitchen and a scrumptious breakfast in the dining room or outdoors in the fresh sea air on one of the porches. Treat yourself to a rarity these days: hand-ironed bed sheets. Learn more on the Web, www.lordmayors.com

Lord Mayor's Bed & Breakfast Inn

435 Cedar Avenue
Long Beach, CA 90802
562-436-0324
Fax 562-436-0324

Hazelnut Squares

"This recipe is very simple and very forgiving," notes Innkeeper Laura Brasser. *"It invites you to experiment with different ingredients and portions. The motivation for developing the recipe was a generous supply of hazelnuts sent to us from Oregon by my sister-in-law. It's delicious as a tea-time dessert."* Makes 9 squares.

$\frac{1}{2}$ cup butter or margarine
$\frac{1}{2}$ cup dark brown sugar, packed
1 cup flour, sifted

Topping

2 eggs
1 cup light brown sugar, packed
$\frac{1}{2}$ cup coconut
1 cup coarsely chopped hazelnuts
2 tablespoons flour
1 teaspoon vanilla extract
$\frac{1}{4}$ teaspoon salt
powdered sugar

- Preheat oven to 350 degrees. Grease an 8 x 8-inch pan.
- With a mixer, cream the butter and brown sugar until light and fluffy. Add the flour and mix well.
- Spread onto the bottom of pan. Bake for 20 minutes.
- To make the topping, beat the eggs until frothy. Gradually add the brown sugar, beating until thick.
- In another bowl, toss together the coconut, nuts, and flour.
- Add the flour mixture, along with the vanilla extract and salt, to the egg mixture; mix well.
- Spread topping over the slightly cooled crust. Bake for 20 more minutes.
- Cool for 15 minutes and cut into 9 squares. Sprinkle with powdered sugar.

Thurston House

*T*hurston House was once the winter getaway for wealthy businessman Cyrus B. Thurston of Minneapolis. Built in 1885, Thurston House has been restored to its original splendor. The pine and cyprus woodwork gleams, boating a magnificent built-in dining room server and wainscotting, original hardwood floors, six beautiful mantels, and wonderful wood paneling.

After 18 years in the corporate world, Carole Ballard was ready for a change. "Going from a Fortune 500 company to being self-employed was a big change, but one for the better!" she notes. Thurston House was completely renovated and opened for business September 15, 1992. Four cozy guestrooms have lake views, a soaking tub or something special in each room. Carole is on hand to tell guests the history of the home, as well as interesting area history.

Located just five miles north of downtown Orlando on five wooded acres, Thurston House's serene atmosphere belies its convenient location. The grounds include over an acre of fruit trees, flowering bushes, and herb and flower gardens. Guests amble through the camellia bushes, hide away on secluded benches, play croquet, or fish from the banks of tranquil Lake Eulalia. Birdwatching is another favorite activity among visitors. In the evening, guests sip wine and visit on the exquisite wrap-around porch.

Carole greets early risers with the aroma of baked goods and fresh brewed coffee. She serves her delectable breakfast by candlelight in the beautifully restored dining room. Learn more on the Web, www.thurstonhouse.com

Thurston House

851 Lake Avenue
Maitland, FL 32751
407-539-1911
800-843-2721
Fax 407-539-0365

Hermit Bars

"Mom used to make these all the time for us kids," recalls Innkeeper Carole Ballard. "The spices are a delicious mix, making these bars delectable with a big glass of milk." Makes 16 to 20 bars.

1¾ cups flour
1 teaspoon cinnamon
½ teaspoon nutmeg
½ teaspoon baking soda
¼ teaspoon ground cloves
½ cup butter
⅔ cup brown sugar, packed
1 egg
¼ cup molasses
½ cup raisins

- Preheat oven to 350 degrees. Grease a 9 x 13-inch pan.
- In a large bowl, whisk together the flour, cinnamon, nutmeg, baking soda and cloves.
- In another bowl, using an electric mixer, cream the butter and brown sugar. Beat in the egg and then the molasses.
- Add the butter mixture to the flour mixture.
- Next, add the raisins and mix well.
- Spread the mixture into pan.
- Bake for 15 minutes.
- Score into squares, and completely cool before removing from pan.

Island Escape Bed & Breakfast

*G*uests at Island Escape revel in privacy — this B&B contains a single suite. The spacious accommodations include a living room finished in Hawaiian decor and a whirlpool bath. This contemporary home overlooks Puget Sound and the Olympic Mountains; a spectacular view of Mount Rainier awaits at the Fox Island bridge, just a short hike away.

Activities in this area of the Pacific Northwest run the gamut from action (scuba diving, windsurfing, sailing, mountain climbing) to total relaxation (beach-combing, bird- and wildlife-watching, reading). Nearby, the quaint fishing village of Gig Harbor hosts a myriad of events throughout the year, including parades, salmon bakes, local theatre productions, Autumn Apple Squeezing, and a summer art festival.

By concentrating on one set of guests at a time, innkeeper Paula Pascoe has found a variety of ways to pamper her visitors. Breakfast is served in the privacy of the suite; Paula features tasty, low-fat cuisine including such specialties as crab, ham, or veggie quiche, homemade granola, whole wheat huckleberry pancakes, and warm quick bread with French butter. She often strolls out to pluck fresh mint sprigs and edible flowers in season to complement the breakfast trays. E-mail address is paula@island-escape.com

Island Escape Bed & Breakfast
210 Island Boulevard
Fox Island, WA 98333
253-549-2044

Island Fruit Bars

"This is a great pick-me-up bar," notes Paula Pascoe, innkeeper. *"We often pack them up for guests to keep in their pockets while they are off for the day exploring the area."* Her husband's daughter, Kim, shared this favorite recipe. Makes 16 to 20 bars.

½ cup unsalted butter, room temperature
1 cup dark brown sugar, packed
1 teaspoon vanilla extract
1 egg, room temperature
1½ cups flour
½ teaspoon salt
½ teaspoon baking powder
½ teaspoon cinnamon
⅛ teaspoon allspice
1 cup plus 2 tablespoons old-fashioned rolled oats
1 cup packed, moist, pitted prunes, finely diced
1 cup packed dried apricots, finely diced
1 cup golden raisins

■ Preheat oven to 350 degrees. Grease a 9 x 13-inch pan.
■ With an electric mixer, cream the butter and brown sugar until light and fluffy. (This will take approximately 3 to 4 minutes).
■ Add the vanilla and egg. Beat for 2 more minutes, until the mixture becomes light in color. (Mixture may look curdled, but it will smooth out).
■ With the mixer on lowest speed, add the flour, salt, baking powder, cinnamon, and allspice. Continue mixing while adding the oats, prunes, apricots, and raisins.
■ Use your hands to pat the dough evenly into pan, pressing down firmly to smooth the dough.
■ Bake for 20 to 25 minutes, or until top is lightly browned, looks dry, and feels soft to the touch.
■ Place pan on a rack to cool. (Bars will firm slightly as they cool.) When cool, cut into squares.

Island Escape Bed & Breakfast

*G*uests at Island Escape revel in privacy — this B&B contains a single suite. The spacious accommodations include a living room finished in Hawaiian decor and a whirlpool bath. This contemporary home overlooks Puget Sound and the Olympic Mountains; a spectacular view of Mount Rainier awaits at the Fox Island bridge, just a short hike away.

Activities in this area of the Pacific Northwest run the gamut from action (scuba diving, windsurfing, sailing, mountain climbing) to total relaxation (beach-combing, bird- and wildlife-watching, reading). Nearby, the quaint fishing village of Gig Harbor hosts a myriad of events throughout the year, including parades, salmon bakes, local theatre productions, Autumn Apple Squeezing, and a summer art festival.

By concentrating on one set of guests at a time, innkeeper Paula Pascoe has found a variety of ways to pamper her visitors. Breakfast is served in the privacy of the suite; Paula features tasty, low-fat cuisine including such specialties as crab, ham, or veggie quiche, homemade granola, whole wheat huckleberry pancakes, and warm quick bread with French butter. She often strolls out to pluck fresh mint sprigs and edible flowers in season to complement the breakfast trays. E-mail address is paula@island-escape.com

Island Escape Bed & Breakfast

210 Island Boulevard
Fox Island, WA 98333
253-549-2044

Johnny Appleseed Cookies

"When my husband was the Air Force ROTC commander at Montana State University in Bozeman, the wife of one of his staff members shared this recipe," said Paula Pascoe, innkeeper. She's been making them for about 15 years now and has printed the popular recipe in her Island Escape cookbook. Makes 4 dozen cookies.

2 cups flour
1 teaspoon baking soda
1 teaspoon cinnamon
½ teaspoon ground cloves
½ teaspoon nutmeg
½ teaspoon salt
⅔ cup golden raisins
⅔ cup sunflower seeds
1 cup brown sugar, packed
½ cup butter, softened
1 egg
¼ cup apple juice
1 large, tart apple

- Preheat oven to 375 degrees. Grease cookie sheets.
- In a large bowl, stir together the flour, baking soda, cinnamon, cloves, nutmeg, and salt.
- In a separate bowl, stir together the raisins and sunflower seeds.
- With an electric mixer, beat brown sugar, butter, and egg until well combined.
- Beat half of the flour mixture into the egg mixture. Next, beat in the apple juice. Finally, beat in the rest of the flour mixture.
- Stir in the raisin mixture by hand; mix well. Then chop the apple and stir.
- Drop by tablespoonfuls (or use a small melon ball scoop) onto cookie sheets.
- Bake for 10 to 12 minutes. Cool on a rack.

Linden Lea on Long Lake

*J*im and Vicky McDonnell took a deteriorating summer cottage and turned it into a contemporary, multilevel B&B with two guestrooms, both with window seats from which to watch the sunset. Guests at this lakeside B&B can work up quite an appetite. They are welcome to swim on the inn's Long Lake beach, fish, or take the rowboat over to one of the islands. After a busy day, visitors are happy to curl up by the fire, where they admire the inn's lovely, solid cherry mantel, hand carved in 1880.

Linden Lea takes its name from the Lake District in England. Long Lake was referred to by Native Americans as the Lake of Many Islands. Multilevel sundecks take guests through the birch trees and ferns to the beach.

The B&B is located minutes from Traverse City, Interlochen Center for the Arts, the Sleeping Bear Dunes National Lakeshore, and other area attractions. Guests come year 'round to enjoy the many Lake Michigan attractions and special packages Vicky has created, such as cooking classes. E-mail address is lindenlea@aol.com

Linden Lea on Long Lake

279 South Long Lake Road
Traverse City, MI 49684
616-943-9182

Linden Scotch-a-Roo Bars

It's hard for the guests and the innkeeper here to resist these bars, a marshmellow-free classic that often shows up at bake sales and potlucks (make sure you note the peanut content for those with allergies!). "I dare you to eat just one!" Vicky McDonnell challenges her guests! Makes 20 to 24 bars.

    1 cup sugar
    1 cup light corn syrup
    1 cup peanut butter
    6 cups crispy rice cereal
    1 package (6 ounces) butterscotch chips
    1 package (6 ounces) semi-sweet chocolate chips

■ Place sugar and corn syrup in a saucepan and bring to a boil, stirring constantly. Boil for 2 minutes.

■ Remove from heat and stir in peanut butter.

■ Measure cereal into a large bowl. Pour syrup mixture over cereal and mix together.

■ Spread mixture into an ungreased 9 x 13-inch pan and press flat.

■ Mix butterscotch and chocolate chips in a microwave-safe bowl and melt. Stir and spread over cereal mixture.

■ When chocolate has hardened, cut into bars.

Old Iron Inn Bed & Breakfast

*T*he Old Iron Inn is located in Aroostook County, in northern Maine, far from the touristed areas along the coast. This area is so unusual that it is simply known as "The County" throughout Maine and much of the rest of New England, explain innkeepers Kate and Kevin McCartney. Visitors will find that "The County" has the largest geographic area but lowest population density in the Eastern United States and is home to several active Swedish communities. Half the population speaks French.

Kate and Kevin opened the inn in 1992, partly because there were few bed and breakfast inns in this scenic area and partly because they enjoy meeting a wide variety of travelers. As part of her studies as an undergraduate, Kate spent a semester in England and traveled around Europe, staying at B&Bs. She enjoyed the experience and has based the Old Iron Inn on the European model, accommodating guests' assorted comfort and dietary needs.

The name of the inn comes from the McCartney's collection of antique irons that decorates the house. They've found irons hold considerable diversity despite their use as an ordinary household appliance. The McCartneys are avid readers, and their specialized libraries include mysteries, books about Abraham Lincoln, and aviation history. The reading room, open to guests, also boasts forty magazine subscriptions. A monthly music night is also open to guests.

The inn is a turn-of-the-century Arts and Crafts style house, with the original interior oak woodwork intact. The McCartneys have made sensitive renovations, striving to maintain its historical integrity. The four guestrooms are each furnished in oak with highback beds. "There is no television on the premises," said Kate. "There are simply too many other things to do."

The Old Iron Inn Bed & Breakfast
155 High Street
Caribou, ME 04736
207-492-4766

Little Lime Bites

"These are pretty little cookies with a sweet-tangy taste that is both unusual and irresistible," said Innkeeper Kate McCartney. "On a cut-glass platter on a buffet table, they steal the show. You may substitute lemon for the lime in the juice and rind, and lemon curd or peach preserves for the lime marmalade. Or, use orange extract and orange rind with orange marmalade." Makes approximately 70 cookies.

1½ cups butter
1½ cups sugar
1 package (8 ounces) cream cheese, softened
2 eggs, room temperature
2 tablespoons lime juice
½ teaspoon grated lime peel, or to taste
4½ cups flour
1½ teaspoons baking powder
English lime marmalade
powdered sugar

- Preheat oven to 350 degrees.
- Beat together butter, sugar, and softened cream cheese, mixing until all is incorporated.
- Beat in the eggs, lime juice, and lime peel.
- Sift the flour with the baking powder; add to the butter mixture, stirring completely. (At this point, dough can be refrigerated; wrap well in plastic and it will keep for up to a week.)
- For each cookie, shape about a tablespoon's worth of dough into a ball. Place on an ungreased cookie sheet. Make a neat well in the center using your thumb. Fill each well with about a ¼-teaspoon's worth of lime marmalade.
- Bake for 12 to 15 minutes. The cookies will not get brown on the top, but the bottom will brown nicely.
- Cool on a wire rack. Sprinkle generously with powdered sugar.

Thorwood and Rosewood Inns

*T*he year was 1983, and in Minnesota, hardly anyone had heard of B&Bs, let alone stayed in one. That was the year that Pam and Dick Thorsen opened two guestrooms in their 1880 home. They had bought the apartment building for their home and to generate a little extra income. But it turned out the Thorsens were perfect for the B&B business: Dick is quite capable of undertaking major historic restoration projects and Pam, the consummate romantic, decorates luxurious suites and entices guests to them. Today they own and operate two historic inns with a total of 15 guestrooms, and the popular inns are often named Minnesota's best and most-romantic getaways. Thorwood, as it is now named, was built as a lumber baron's home in this Mississippi rivertown. Eventually, it was turned into a private hospital and then an apartment house. After unending work, it now has seven guestrooms on three floors, all with fireplaces and/or whirlpools. In 1986, they purchased another historic home that once served as a hospital. Rosewood, owned by the city and in disrepair, was "gutted" to the studs and rebuilt with eight luxurious suites and a gift shop on the back porch. Guests can sequester themselves in luxury, ordering hat box suppers on the weekends, or breakfast served in their suites or in formal dining spaces. Or they can stroll downtown for dinner and coffee. Located only a half-hour from St. Paul, Hastings has a winery, nature center, antique stores, two coffee shops, a toy store, a Scandinavian shop, and a well-loved restaurant, all in town or nearby.

Pam, who is active in historic preservation efforts in the city, creates several special packages and theme weekends. Learn more on the Web, www.thorwoodinn.com

Thorwood and Rosewood Inns

315 Pine Street
Hastings, MN 55033
651-437-3297 ■ Fax 651-437-4129

Maggie Lee's Sugar Cookies

These cookies were first made famous in 1976, when they were baked for Bicentennial Coffees held around the state. They are from Maggie Lee, a newspaper woman and tour guide in Stillwater, Minn., the state's oldest town. Hazel Jacobsen, Hastings historian and friend of Innkeeper Pam Thorsen, provided Pam with the recipe to serve to her guests. "Guests are often surprised that the cookies are soft, instead of crunchy," Pam said. Makes approximately 3 dozen cookies.

1 cup sugar
½ cup dark brown sugar, packed
½ cup butter-flavored shortening
½ cup butter
1 egg
1 teaspoon vanilla extract
2½ cups sifted flour
2 teaspoons baking soda
2 teaspoons cream of tartar
½ teaspoon salt
extra sugar

- With an electric mixer, beat together sugar, brown sugar, shortening and butter.
- Beat in egg and vanilla.
- Slowly beat in flour, baking soda, cream of tartar and salt.
- Preheat oven to 350 degrees and grease cookie sheets.
- Roll dough into 1-inch balls, then roll the balls in the extra sugar.
- Place dough on cookie sheets. Bake for 10 to 11 minutes or until slightly browned and set.

Inn on the Rio

*L*ocated on the Rio Fernando at the base of the Sangre de Cristo Mountains, just east from historic downtown Taos Plaza, the Inn on the Rio has recently been re-born. Innkeepers Robert and Julie Chahalane left the corporate "rat race" back in New England and took on the monumental task of bringing a former landmark back into its glory. Julie, with a master's degree in nutrition, knew she could satisfy her guests' hunger for healthy Southwest treats. Robert, a retired marketing executive with an background in finance and economics, knew he could make the numbers work. But what about the declining physical structures? New friends and neighbors, happy to see the interest of the new innkeepers, offered their knowledge, and the task began.

One renovation highlight is an outdoor, in-ground hot tub that offers a spectacular view of Taos Mountain during the day and the star-studded sky at night. Rooms are decorated in "cowboy casual" and "pueblo picturesque" with blankets, rugs, and art collected from all over New Mexico. Julie's new flowerbeds are filled with hollyhocks, Mexican Hats, and other native plants. The "icing on the cake" has been visits by two Southwest artists who spent several weeks painting murals on the exterior walls, arches over the doorways, and, with painstaking detail, the interiors, including each bathroom! In front of the historic Carmen Valarde Kiva fireplace in the inn's cozy gathering room, Julie offers guests suggestions for dining, sightseeing, and shopping. Robert, an outdoor enthusiast, reveals the best-kept secrets of the great outdoors for close-by hiking, mountain biking, and challenging skiing. Learn more on the Web, www.innontherio.com

Inn on the Rio
Box 6529-NDCBU
910 East Kit Carson Road
Taos, NM 87571
505-758-7199 ■ Fax 505-751-1816
Toll-free 800-859-6752

Mexican Wedding Cakes

These traditional cookies are known by many different names, but they are always served when a family would get together for a wedding, funeral or baptism, said Innkeeper Julie Cahalane. "Nothing makes the inn smell as warm and wonderful as a batch of Mexican Wedding Cakes baking in the oven." Her guests inhale the rich cookie. Makes 6 dozen cookies.

> 2 cups butter
> 1 cup powdered sugar
> 2 teaspoons vanilla extract
> 4½ cups flour
> 2 cups chopped pecans
> additional powdered sugar

- Preheat oven to 325 degrees. Grease cookie sheets.
- With an electric mixer, cream the butter, powdered sugar, and vanilla.
- Beat in the flour and pecans.
- Roll stiff dough into bite-sized balls. Place 8 across and 9 down on a cookie sheet.
- Bake for 20 minutes.
- After cooling for 5 minutes, roll still-warm cookies in a bowl of powdered sugar. Allow to cool.
- Roll again to cover completely.

Lord Mayor's
Bed & Breakfast Inn

*T*his elegant Edwardian house was the home of the first mayor of Long Beach, Charles H. Windham. His unofficial Edwardian-style title, Lord Mayor, was bestowed by British beauty contestants enjoying the amenities of this seaside resort in the mid-1900s. The Lord Mayor's house was meticulously restored by historians Reuben and Laura Brasser and received the prestigious 1992 Great American Home Award from the National Trust for Historic Preservation for sensitivity in restoration of an historic house.

Their inn has expanded into a collection comprising a total of 12 rooms, with other rooms located in the Cinnamon House, the Apple House and the Garden House. The Garden House was converted from the original horse barn and the others are 1908 city cottages near the original mayor's home.

Located in the heart of Long Beach, Lord Mayor's Inn is close to many major businesses, shopping, dining, and leisure activities. Within walking distance are city and state government offices, the World Trade Center, the Convention Center, Farmers Market, and the Blue Line rapid transit.

Gracious hospitality awaits guests in the Brassers' home. These innkeepers have a reputation for friendliness and fabulous food. Enjoy coffee in the kitchen and a scrumptious breakfast in the dining room or outdoors in the fresh sea air on one of the porches. Treat yourself to a rarity these days: hand-ironed bed sheets. Learn more on the Web, www.lordmayors.com

Lord Mayor's Bed & Breakfast Inn

435 Cedar Avenue
Long Beach, CA 90802
562-436-0324
Fax 562-436-0324

Molasses Applesauce Cookies

"This soft cookie recipe was first used at the Inn when Margarita de La Gardia came to visit us in 1989," recalled Innkeeper Laura Brasser. "She was the daughter of the Mayor and Mrs. C.H. Windham and was the baby of the family when they moved here in 1904. Through telephone conversations, I learned of her love for these cookies." Makes 60 cookies.

½ cup butter-flavored shortening
½ cup sugar
½ cup molasses
1 egg
2 cups flour
2 teaspoons cinnamon
1 teaspoon baking soda
1 teaspoon salt
½ teaspoon ground cloves
1 cup applesauce
½ cup chopped raisins
½ cup chopped nuts

- Preheat oven to 350 degrees. Lightly grease cookie sheets.
- With an electric mixer, cream the shortening and sugar until fluffy. Add the molasses. Beat in the egg.
- In a separate bowl, stir together the flour, cinnamon, baking soda, salt and cloves. Beat into the molasses mixture.
- Blend in the applesauce, raisins, and nuts.
- Drop dough by teaspoonfuls onto cookie sheet, leaving room for cookies to spread.
- Bake for 12 to 15 minutes, or until browned. Remove and cool.

Lord Mayor's Bed & Breakfast Inn

*T*his elegant Edwardian house was the home of the first mayor of Long Beach, Charles H. Windham. His unofficial Edwardian-style title, Lord Mayor, was bestowed by British beauty contestants enjoying the amenities of this seaside resort in the mid-1900s. The Lord Mayor's house was meticulously restored by historians Reuben and Laura Brasser and received the prestigious 1992 Great American Home Award from the National Trust for Historic Preservation for sensitivity in restoration of an historic house.

Their inn has expanded into a collection comprising a total of 12 rooms, with other rooms located in the Cinnamon House, the Apple House and the Garden House. The Garden House was converted from the original horse barn and the others are 1908 city cottages near the original mayor's home.

Located in the heart of Long Beach, Lord Mayor's Inn is close to many major businesses, shopping, dining, and leisure activities. Within walking distance are city and state government offices, the World Trade Center, the Convention Center, Farmers Market, and the Blue Line rapid transit.

Gracious hospitality awaits guests in the Brassers' home. These innkeepers have a reputation for friendliness and fabulous food. Enjoy coffee in the kitchen and a scrumptious breakfast in the dining room or outdoors in the fresh sea air on one of the porches. Treat yourself to a rarity these days: hand-ironed bed sheets. Learn more on the Web, www.lordmayors.com

Lord Mayor's Bed & Breakfast Inn
435 Cedar Avenue
Long Beach, CA 90802
562-436-0324
Fax 562-436-0324

Molasses Planks

These cookies are an unusual shape that often delight guests. "At the Inn, we present them standing upright in an antique celery keeper," said Laura Brasser, innkeeper. "Guests are encouraged to break off what they wish, or enjoy the entire 'plank'!" Makes 3 dozen cookies.

         2 tablespoons butter
    ½ cup brown sugar, packed
    ½ cup molasses
         1 teaspoon lemon extract
    ⅓ cup buttermilk
         3 cups flour
    ½ teaspoon salt
    ½ teaspoon ginger
    ½ teaspoon cinnamon
    ½ teaspoon ground cloves
    ½ teaspoon baking soda

- With an electric mixer, cream the butter, brown sugar, and molasses until fluffy.
- In a small bowl, whisk together the lemon flavoring and buttermilk.
- In another bowl, sift together the flour, salt, ginger, cinnamon, cloves, and baking soda.
- Alternately beat the liquid and dry ingredients into the creamed mixture; blend well.
- Split dough in half and roll each half into a ball. Wrap in plastic wrap and chill for several hours or overnight. (May be refrigerated for several days.)
- When ready to bake, preheat oven to 350 degrees. Grease cookie sheets.
- Flour a board and roll each ball into a rectangle approximately ¼ inch thick.
- Transfer dough to cookie sheets. Cut into 1¼-inch wide strips and separate slightly. Bake for 12 to 15 minutes.
- Cool and break planks into desired length.

Watch Hill Bed & Breakfast

*W*hen guests come to Barbara Lauterbach's B&B, they may come for many reasons — but when they come *back*, "food" is always one that draws them. A gourmet chef, Barbara trained at renowned culinary institutes in Paris, Italy, and England. Her food-related career has included developing cooking schools for a chain of department stores, serving as an instructor at the New England Culinary Institute, and acting as a consultant and spokesperson for food-related businesses. She also has done regular television cooking segments and presents classes around the country. When she bought the B&B in 1989, her background was just one of the talents that made innkeeping attractive to her. Guests love to sit and chat during an excellent breakfast, and Barbara holds cooking classes at the B&B.

Watch Hill is one of the oldest homes in Center Harbor. Built circa 1772 by the brother of the town's founder, it has views of Lake Winnipesaukee, just down the street. Guests in the four guestrooms especially enjoy the home's porch in the summer or warming up with a mug of hot cider after skiing or snowmobiling in the winter. Barbara's full country breakfast often showcases New Hampshire products and may feature fresh, hot breads, sausage, bacon, home-fries, fresh fruit, and brown eggs. Guests enjoy the food and the conversation, which often turns to the how her B&B was named (after the champion bull mastiffs Barbara used to raise from the Watch Hill kennel in Cincinnati, Ohio). Watch Hill is a five-minute walk from one of the country's foremost quilt shops, and quilters are frequent guests. "Sometimes they come in vans and take over the whole place!" Barbara said. "They have Show and Tell in the evening, inspecting each other's purchases of fabrics and patterns."

Watch Hill Bed & Breakfast

P.O. Box 1605
Center Harbor, NH 03226
603-253-4334
Fax 603-253-8560

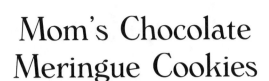

Mom's Chocolate Meringue Cookies

"I never serve these without being asked the recipe," said Innkeeper Barbara Lauterbach. "They will keep in a tin cookie cannister for a day or two, but it is highly unlikely you'll have any left." Makes approximately 18 cookies.

> 2 egg whites
> ½ cup sugar
> 1 package (6 ounces) semi-sweet chocolate chips, melted and cooled
> ½ teaspoon vanilla extract
> ¾ cup chopped walnuts or pecans

■ Preheat oven to 350 degrees. Grease and lightly flour cookie sheet.
■ With an electric mixer, beat egg whites until almost stiff.
■ Slowly add sugar. Beat mixture until stiff and smooth.
■ Fold cooled chocolate, vanilla, and nuts into egg mixture.
■ Drop by spoonfuls, 2 inches apart, on cookie sheet. Bake for 12 minutes.
■ Cool for 2 minutes, then remove to a cookie rack.

The Settlement at Round Top

*L*arry and Karen Beever's Settlement at Round Top is an historical treasure set on 35 acres in the lush green, gently rolling hills of east central Texas. "We strive to make it a place where guests can enjoy times past in the ease of today's comfort," Karen said.

The innkeepers spent their honeymoon in Europe and fell in love with the bed and breakfast concept. "It was just natural that when we found a Civil War-era homestead so run down that our realtor refused to show it to us, that we ultimately decided to share our restored treasure," Karen said. They also brought in additional pioneer log cabins and cottages scheduled to be torn down. Their renovation and restoration efforts have turned them into antique-filled guest accommodations with fireplaces, whirlpools and porches.

A large notched and pegged Civil War-era barn is the unique setting for the full breakfasts, served with a flare by Larry and Karen. The barn also is available for conferences and retreats. The setting is full of deer, birds, miniature roses, centuries-old oak trees, split rail fences, miniature horses, and, in season, the wildflowers for which Texas is famous. Karen and Larry are active members of the Historic Accommodations of Texas and the prestigious Independent Innkeepers Association and the Settlement was featured in the June 1997 *Country Living Magazine*. Learn more on the Web, www.thesettlement.com

The Settlement at Round Top
P.O. Box 176
Round Top, TX 78954
409-249-5015
Fax 409-249-5587
Toll-free 888-ROUNDTOP

Mom's Norwegian Spritz Cookies

"Coming from a large family in North Dakota, many a cold winter day was spent baking for friends and family," said Innkeeper Karen Beevers. *"Mom would crank out these cookies by the hundreds, the cookie press form reflecting the event of the season. For really special events, she would add food coloring to the dough and a red-hot cinnamon candy strategically placed!"* Makes about 80 cookies, depending on the cookie press form used.

         2   cups butter
      1 ½   cups sugar
         2   eggs
         2   teaspoons almond extract
         1   teaspoon baking powder
         ¼   teaspoon salt
         5   cups flour

■ Preheat oven to 350 degrees. Lighltly grease cookie sheets.
■ With an electric mixer, combine the butter, sugar, eggs, almond extract, baking powder, salt and flour. Chill the dough.
■ When chilled, push the dough through a cookie press onto cookie sheets.
■ Bake for 10 to 12 minutes. Watch carefully during final baking period so they don't brown.

The Lamplighter Bed & Breakfast

*J*udy and Heinz Bertram and their cocker spaniel, Freddy, welcome recreational and business travelers to their Queen Anne-style home, which was built in 1895 by a local doctor as his home and office. After living for more than twenty years in Germany and traveling extensively throughout Europe, the Bertrams brought their collection of fine antiques and original paintings and lithographs to their Michigan B&B.

They purchased their "dream B&B" virtually overnight, Judy said. She and Heinz added a deck with a gazebo and a red brick patio and extensive landscaping so that summer guests can enjoy refreshments outside. Judy is a Michigan native and former administrator in the Department of Defense school system overseas, and Heinz, originally from Germany, is a retired U.S. Air Force officer.

Breakfast may be served on the patio, in the gazebo, or in the formal dining room, depending on the season. Afterwards, guests might head off to swim in Lake Michigan, stroll along its miles of sandy beaches, walk to the lighthouse at the entrance to Ludington harbor, or shop for antiques. Guests find plenty of outdoor activities year 'round, including biking through Ludington State Park, rated one of the state's best, skiing on miles of groomed cross-country trails, or hiking or strolling along nature trails. Judy and Heinz are happy to help guests plan their itinerary to explore scenic Western Michigan. Learn more on the Web, www.laketolake.com/lamplighter

The Lamplighter
602 East Ludington Avenue
Ludington, MI 49431
616-843-9792
Fax 616-845-6070

No-Bake Chocolate Oatmeal Cookies

The ingredients for these fudge-like cookies usually are available in the pantry, and they are quick and easy, with or without the nuts or coconut. "They also taught Heinz a valuable lesson — to follow recipes to the letter," reported Judy Bertram about her husband and co-innkeeper. "He tried a short-cut by only heating the mixture, instead of boiling it for the required time, and ended up with a sticky mess!" Makes 5 to 6 dozen cookies.

> ½ cup butter
> 2 cups sugar
> ¼ cup light corn syrup
> 6 tablespoons unsweetened cocoa
> ½ cup evaporated milk
> 3 cups quick-cooking or old-fashioned rolled oats
> ½ cup chopped nuts
> ½ cup coconut
> 1 teaspoon vanilla extract

- In a large saucepan over medium-high heat, whisk together the butter, sugar, corn syrup, cocoa, and evaporated milk.
- Bring mixture to a boil and boil at least 2 minutes, stirring constantly, or until a soft ball forms.
- Remove from heat and stir in the oats, chopped nuts, coconut, and vanilla. Mix well.
- Drop dough by spoonfuls onto waxed paper. Store in a tightly sealed container.

The Old Miners' Lodge

*O*ld Miners' Lodge was originally established by E. P. Ferry as lodging for single miners working his Woodside mine, located on "Treasure Mountain" behind the building. The first building, circa 1889, was two story, with dorm-style rooms, a kitchen shanty off the back, and an outhouse and blacksmith's barn behind. The Lodge was built with lumber salvaged from the surrounding mines. Electricity was added in 1912, and indoor plumbing around 1919. In the early 1920s, the Lodge was changed to married miners' housing, and converted into a number of tiny apartments.

In 1983, Hugh Daniels and Susan Wynne purchased the Lodge and surrounding property and began restoration. Hugh and Susan opened "The Old Miners' Lodge" with five guestrooms, then added two more, and then, in 1988, added a fourth section of the building, making 12 guestrooms in all. The guestrooms are all named after Park City mining era personalities, and decorated in period style. Creature comforts, such as down comforters and a hot tub under the stars, have not been overlooked. The Lodge is now owned by Jon Brinton, who built an innkeeper's cottage next door. Hugh is general manager, also overseeing the 1904 Imperior Hotel, the Lodge's sister property. Susan, Liza Simpson and Kristin Sohrweide greet guests each morning with a hearty full breakfast, fresh coffee, teas and nectars. The Lodge is in Park City's Historic District, an easy walk to Main Street shopping and dining. The Park City Mountain Resort "town lift" is a block away, and guests can ski right into the Lodge's backyard! Park City is now a year 'round resort, with horseback riding, golf, and mountain biking in the summer. Learn more on the Web, www.oldminerslodge.com

The Old Miners' Lodge

615 Woodside Avenue
P.O. Box 2639
Park City, UT 84060
435-645-8068 ■ Fax 435-645-7420

Oatmeal Cookies

These are chewy, dense cookies "that will be sure to fill you up," notes Liza Simpson, who jokingly refers to herself as the Lodge's "kitchen goddess." She often gives these to guests who have to leave too early to enjoy the Lodge's full breakfast. She uses a #24-size cookie or ice cream scoop, which equals two tablespoons in size, and makes the finished cookies about 3 inches across. Makes 36 cookies.

$1\frac{1}{2}$ cups butter, softened but still firm
$1\frac{1}{3}$ cups light brown sugar, packed
$1\frac{1}{3}$ cups sugar
  3 eggs
  2 cups flour
  1 teaspoon freshly grated nutmeg
$\frac{1}{2}$ teaspoon salt
$\frac{1}{2}$ teaspoon baking powder
$4\frac{1}{2}$ cups old-fashioned rolled oats
$2\frac{1}{4}$ cups dried cranberries, optional

- Preheat oven to 350 degrees. Lightly grease cookie sheets, or use parchment paper.
- With an electric mixer, cream the butter. Add the brown sugar and sugar and beat until fluffy, about 3 minutes.
- Beat in eggs, one at a time.
- In another bowl, combine the flour, nutmeg, salt and baking powder. Add to the butter mixture and mix gently.
- Mix in the oats and fruit, by hand, if necessary.
- Place dough on pan using a cookie scoop. Flatten slightly.
- Bake for 8 minutes and rotate pan. Bake an additional 8 minutes (do not over bake!). Edges should be brown, but the rest of the cookie should still be quite light in color.

Yankee Hill Inn Bed & Breakfast

*T*he ambiance of quiet, small town life in the heart of the Kettle Moraine recreational area is what Yankee Hill Inn Bed and Breakfast Innkeepers Peg and Jim Stahlman find draws guests to their two historic homes-turned-B&Bs.

Yankee Hill Inn B&B is comprised of two historic homes restored by the Stahlmans. One is a Sheboygan County landmark, a Queen Anne Victorian–style, built in 1891. The other is an 1870 Gothic Italianate listed on the National Register of Historic Places. Both were built in the "Yankee Hill" area of Plymouth by hard-working, affluent brothers, Henry and Gilbert Huson.

Yankee Hill Inn has 12 guestrooms, decorated with period antiques and other touches to reflect historic lodging. Six guestrooms have single whirlpool tubs. Landscaped yards, parlors, fireplaces, and an enclosed front porch allow the guests to gather and relax. Each morning, guests wake up to the aroma of a full breakfast, featuring home-baked muffins and breads, and the cookie jar is open to guests.

From the Inn, guests take a short walk through Huson Park and across the Mullet River footbridge into downtown Plymouth, where they can explore charming antique and gift shops and dine in excellent restaurants. At the Plymouth Center is an art gallery, the Plymouth Historical Museum, and visitor information.

Outdoor adventures surround Plymouth in the glacially sculpted terrain. Enjoy the Kettle Moraine State Forest, many lakes, marked nature trails and the Ice Age Trail for hiking and biking. The paved Old Plank Road recreational trail, historic Plymouth walking tour, Road America race track and the Kohler Design Center, featuring the latest in Kohler bathroom and kitchen ideas, are also popular. Sheboygan and Lake Michigan are just 15 minutes away. Learn more on the Web, www.yankeehillinn.com

Yankee Hill Inn Bed & Breakfast

405 Collins Street
Plymouth, WI 53073
920-892-2222 ■ Fax 920-892-6228

Oatmeal Jelly Bars

What a sinfully delicious way to "eat your oatmeal"! "This recipe goes together quickly and is a pleasure to serve to guests and family alike," Innkeeper Peg Stahlman reports. These are rich, so halve the recipe and use an 8 x 8-inch pan, if you wish. Makes 24 bars.

  4 cups old-fashioned rolled oats
  2 cups flour
1½ cups brown sugar, packed
  ½ teaspoon salt
1½ cups butter-flavored shortening
  2 cups raspberry jelly (or use your preferred flavor)

- Preheat oven to 350 degrees. Grease a 9 x 13-inch pan.
- Using your fingertips, thoroughly mix the oats, flour, brown sugar, salt, and shortening.
- Pat half of mixture into bottom of pan.
- Spread jelly evenly over dough.
- Sprinkle remaining dough over jelly. Lightly flatten with fingertips.
- Bake for 25 to 30 minutes, or until golden.
- Cool in pan on rack and cut into bars.

White Swan Guest House

*F*rom the exquisite English country gardens that produce fruit and berries for the breakfast table, one might never guess that Innkeeper (and gardener) Peter Goldfarb moved here from Manhattan. But Peter, whose former career was interior design and contracting, has the proverbial green thumb. When combined with the Skagit Valley's fertile farmland, the result is a gorgeous garden. The fertile farmland was just about claiming this 1898 Queen Anne Victorian farmhouse when Peter found it in 1986. It was literally sinking into the ground, having fallen into disrepair in the 1940s. Using historic photos as guides, he undertook the one-year restoration himself. He transformed the farmhouse into a bright, cheery haven, with a new old-fashioned porch. Many of the rooms have views of the Cascade Mountains, Mt. Baker, and the Olympic Mountain range. The farmhouse offers three inviting guestrooms, a woodstove in the parlor, wicker chairs on the back porch, and a tempting platter of cookies waiting on the sideboard. Or guests might choose the Garden Cottage, a romantic hideaway under the trees with a private sun deck.

Peter serves a wholesome, home-cooked, Country Continental breakfast, featuring Pacific Northwest specialties, which might plenty of local fruit such as blackberries, strawberries, raspberries, and peaches. His Old-Fashioned Chocolate Chip Cookies are the guests' all-time favorite and usually are on hand to welcome guests back from their day's adventures. Guests might spend the day bike riding on the back roads, bird watching, or walking along the Skagit River, which runs in front of the house. Just a stone's throw away are the area's renown tulip fields, where thousands come every spring to see the bulb-producing fields in bloom. The towns of LaConner and Mount Vernon, with excellent shopping and dining, and the San Juan Island ferries (in Anacortes) are also nearby. Learn more on the Web, www.cnw.com/~wswan/

The White Swan Guest House

15872 Moore Road
Mount Vernon, WA 98273
360-445-6805

Old-Fashioned Chocolate Chip Cookies

Peter Goldfarb noted that "after 10 years, I can make these in my sleep." He added that chilling this "basic but oh so popular!" cookie dough for an hour or two makes a fatter, crisper cookie. He has tried different variations, including adding oats and nuts, but this is the most reliable — and everyone's favorite. Makes 7 dozen cookies.

$2\frac{1}{2}$ cups flour
1 teaspoon baking soda
1 teaspoon salt
1 cup butter-flavored shortening
$\frac{3}{4}$ cup brown sugar, packed
$\frac{3}{4}$ cup sugar
1 tablespoon vanilla extract
2 eggs
2 cups semi-sweet chocolate chips

- Preheat oven to 375 degrees.
- In a large bowl, sift together the flour, baking soda, and salt.
- With an electric mixer, beat the shortening, brown sugar, sugar, and vanilla until light and fluffy. Add the eggs, one at a time. Beat well.
- Add the flour mixture to the sugar mixture, beating until smooth. Stir in the chocolate chips by hand. ("At this point, you can cover and chill dough for 1 to 2 hours, if you like.")
- Using a teaspoon, spoon dough onto an ungreased cookie sheet.
- Bake for 7 to 10 minutes until cookies just turn golden brown. Do not overbake.

Isaiah Hall Bed & Breakfast Inn

*T*ucked away on a quiet street in Cape Cod, this roomy 1857 farmhouse was originally home to Isaiah B. Hall, builder and barrel maker. Rooms in the Main House and the Carriage House have been open to overnight guests since 1948. Innkeeper Marie Brophy offers 10 guestrooms, decorated with oriental rugs and pine or oak cottage antiques.

Visitors sleep on antique iron and brass beds warmed by quilts and awake to Marie's hearty breakfast of homebaked breads and muffins. They follow this repast with a leisurely walk in the gardens, a stroll on the beach, or a visit to nearby cranberry bogs.

Located in the heart of the Cape, Dennis Village offers a handy home base for day trips to points of interest from Provincetown to Plymouth and the popular islands of Cape Cod. The location is perfect for exploring all the Cape has to offer in under an hour. Stroll to Corporation Beach, the Cape's oldest cultivated cranberry bog, and the village's antique and craft shops and excellent restaurants. Or visit the Cape Museum of Fine Arts and the oldest summer theater in America, just around the block. Bike trails, tennis, golf and whalewatching are close by. Learn more on the Web, www.virtualcapecod.com/isaiahhall

Isaiah Hall Bed & Breakfast Inn

152 Whig Street
P.O. Box 1007
Dennis, MA 02638
508-385-9928
800-736-0160
Fax 508-385-5879

Old-Fashioned Peanut Butter Cookies

"This recipe was given to me a long time ago by a former guest," said Innkeeper Marie Brophy. Makes about 4 dozen cookies.

>   1 cup butter-flavored shortening
>   1 cup brown sugar, packed
>   1 cup sugar
>   1 cup peanut butter
>   2 eggs
>   1 teaspoon vanilla extract
>   2½ cups flour
>   ½ teaspoon salt
>   2 teaspoons baking soda

- Preheat oven to 375 degrees.
- With an electric mixer, cream the shortening, brown sugar, sugar, and peanut butter. Add the eggs and vanilla; beat well.
- In a separate bowl, sift the flour, salt, and baking soda. Add to the egg mixture, and mix well.
- Roll the dough into small balls and place on an ungreased cookie sheet.
- Press down on each ball with the tines of a fork.
- Bake for 8 to 10 minutes or until cookies appear set.
- Remove from oven, cool for a few minutes, and remove cookies to cooling racks.

Justin Trails Country Inn

A third-generation dairy farm, the Justin Trails Country Inn property has been in the Justin family since 1914. In 1985, Don and Donna Justin opened ten kilometers of cross-country ski trails, and the B&B opened a year later. The award-winning Justin Trails is set among the scenic wooded hills and valleys of southwestern Wisconsin, near Sparta. The cozy 1920s farmhouse with four guestrooms is complemented by three private luxury cottages: the Granary, the Little House on the Prairie, and the Paul Bunyan — the last two are log cabins. All the rooms are decorated in a romantic country style with such special touches as hand-crafted log furnishings, Amish hickory rocking chairs, stone fireplaces, and painted pine floors.

Donna treats her guests, hungry from the previous day's worth of outdoor activities, to a four-course breakfast that features homemade muffins, granola, yogurt, applesauce or fresh fruit, an entrée, and of course coffee, tea, and juice. A recent addition at Justin Trails is The Eatery, featuring gourmet regional and vegetarian cuisine and a cozy conversation area. But that will soon be turned into something else because the Justins are converting the dairy barn to serve as the restaurant and additional lodging. Area attractions include 12½ kilometers of private, groomed cross-country ski trails, snowtubing, snowshoeing, hiking, biking on the Elroy-Sparta Trail, canoeing, and visiting the nearby Amish community, state and national parks and forests, and quaint antique shops. Guests are encouraged to play with the rabbits, kittens, Peter the pygmy goat, and chickens. The Justins offer special weekend getaways throughout the year, such as family fun packages, ski fests, and women's retreats. Learn more on the Web, www.justintrails.com

Justin Trails Country Inn
7452 Kathryn Avenue on Co. J
Sparta, WI 54656
608-269-4522 ■ Fax 608-269-3280
Toll-free 800-488-4521

Olga's Chewy Oatmeal Cookies

"Olga McAnulty is my friend and an avid bicyclist," said Innkeeper Donna Justin. She bikes all over, and completed 48 days of riding on the 1898 TransAmerica ride and rode 200 miles in the Iditasport in Alaska one February. On the Monroe County (Wisconsin) Century Challenge, held each August, she is also known for the batches of these cookies she makes for the rest stops. Makes approximately 28 cookies.

　　1　cup butter
　　2　cups brown sugar, packed
　　2　teaspoons vanilla extract
　　4　eggs
　　2　cups flour
　1½　teaspoons baking soda
　　1　teaspoon cinnamon
　　½　teaspoon nutmeg
　　4　cups old-fashioned rolled oats
　　1　cup semi-sweet chocolate chips
　　1　cup craisins (dried cranberries)

- Preheat oven to 350 degrees.
- With an electric mixer, cream the butter, brown sugar, and vanilla until smooth. Add the eggs, and beat well.
- In another bowl, mix the flour, baking soda, cinnamon, nutmeg, oats, chocolate chips, and craisins.
- Add the dry ingredients, one third at a time, to the batter until blended.
- Drop dough by teaspoonfuls or a standard-sized ice cream scoop onto a cookie sheet.
- Bake for 12 to 15 minutes.

McKenzie View Bed & Breakfast

*W*hen Roberta and Scott Bolling decided to buy a bed and breakfast, they thought they would find something in Ohio where they had lived for 27 years. The move to Oregon eventually came after a trip to bring their youngest daughter to look at the University of Oregon in Eugene. "Most people couldn't believe we were doing this," Roberta said, "but everything just fell into place so perfectly that we knew it was meant to be."

Buying a private home and starting the B&B from there allowed them to grow into the business and adjust to a new way of life. The job of running a four guestroom B&B on six acres "has been more than a trade-off for previous corporate careers, but it is offset by the rewards of working for yourself," she noted. "This place is too special not to share it, and the guests make it all worthwhile," Scott said.

The four guestrooms are comfortably decorated, and common areas provide space for guests to socialize and relax. The grounds have decks, patios, a gazebo and hammocks scattered throughout to take advantage of the views of extensive perennial gardens and of the river. In most places, the McKenzie is a rushing river, boardered with rocks, that is a gorgeous turquoise color that absolutely capitivates those who see it. Some the nation's finest nurseries are located in the Willamette Valley, along with great hiking, biking, wine tasting, fishing and rafting. University of Oregon sports and cultural activities, along with the Bach Festival and various local celebrations, bring many people to the area. McKenzie View offers a unique setting and atmosphere from which to "do it all." Their motto: "The only thing we overlook is the McKenzie River." Learn more on the Web, http://design-web.com/McKenzieView

McKenzie View Bed & Breakfast
34922 McKenzie View Drive
Springfield, OR 97478
541-726-3887
Fax 541-726-6968

Orange-Cranberry Oatmeal Cookies

At check-in, guests are shown the McKenzie View's cookie jar, which is kept stocked with homemade cookies. "As the B&B becomes more popular, the job of keeping the jar full has become more challenging!" notes Innkeeper Roberta Bolling. "This variation of the traditional oatmeal cookie is always popular." Makes 70 cookies.

¾ cup shortening
1 cup brown sugar, packed
½ cup sugar
1 egg
¼ cup orange juice
1 teaspoon vanilla extract
½ cup chopped dried cranberries
½ teaspoon dried orange peel
3 cups old-fashioned rolled oats
1 cup flour
1 teaspoon salt
½ teaspoon baking soda

- Preheat oven to 350 degrees.
- With an electric mixer, cream the shortening, brown sugar, and sugar. Beat in the egg, orange juice, vanilla, cranberries and orange peel.
- In a separate bowl, stir together the oats, flour, salt, and baking soda. Beat into the sugar mixture to form the dough.
- Drop by teaspoonfuls onto an ungreased cookie sheet.
- Bake for 12 to 15 minutes.

White Mountain Lodge

Charlie and Mary Bast welcome guests to White Mountain Lodge with true Southwestern hospitality. The Lodge, considered the oldest building still standing in the Greer Basin, was built in 1892 as a family home. The two-story log house, constructed of timbers from the area, served mainly as the summer residence of the William Lund family, one of the first Mormon families to settle in Greer.

In 1904, the house was passed on to Lund's son, Marion, upon his marriage. Marion and Agnes, his spouse, converted the home into a year 'round residence, farming, raising eight children and adding onto the house as needed. When Marion retired from farming in 1940, the property was sold and transformed into the White Mountain Lodge by the new owners. Mary and Charlie left administrative positions in Tucson and bought the lodge and began renovation and remodeling in 1993. Each of the seven guestrooms is decorated in a Southwestern country style. The common rooms reflect the home's Southwest country heritage with period antiques, Southwest art and mission style furniture. A rock fireplace is a central feature of the living room. Also available for visitors are full housekeeping cabins, overlooking a gorgeous meadow and the Little Colorado River. Nestled in a remote mountain valley, Greer rarely sees summer temperatures above 76 degrees. The Greer Recreation Area offers opportunities for just about any outdoor activity, from hiking and fishing to downhill and cross-country skiing. And those seeking to do more than just savor a mountain retreat love the Lodge's Murder Mystery Weekends. The Basts offer an exceptional made-from-scratch breakfast each morning. In the evening guests are treated to refreshments and homemade treats, and the cookie jar at White Mountain Lodge is always full. Learn more on the Web, www.wmonline.com/wmlodge

White Mountain Lodge

P.O. Box 143
140 Main Street
Greer, AZ 85927
520-735-7568 ■ Fax 520-735-7498

Orange-Spice Snickerdoodles

"Years ago, a friend gave me a basic recipe for Snickerdoodles," recalls Mary Bast, inn-keeper. *"I decided that it needed a little extra flavor and started adding orange peel and spices."* The change has only earned compliments, and the same recipe that once delighted her children is now enjoyed by her grandchildren, as well as guests. Makes 4 dozen cookies.

    1 cup butter-flavored shortening
1 ½ cups sugar
    2 eggs, beaten
    3 teaspoons baking powder
    1 teaspoon baking soda
    ½ teaspoon salt
    ½ teaspoon nutmeg
    2 tablespoons freshly grated orange peel (or 2 teaspoons dried orange peel)
    1 teaspoon vanilla extract
2 ¾ cups flour
    ½ cup sugar
    ¼ teaspoon nutmeg
    1 teaspoon cinnamon

- Preheat oven to 375 degrees.
- With an electric mixer, beat together the shortening and 1 ½ cups sugar. Add the eggs and beat until creamy.
- Beat in the baking powder, baking soda, salt, nutmeg, orange peel, and vanilla extract; blend well.
- Beat in the flour and mix until no trace of flour remains.
- Roll dough into 1-inch balls.
- In a small bowl, mix together ½ cup sugar, nutmeg, and cinnamon. Dip the dough balls in the sugar mixture.
- Place balls on an ungreased cookie sheet. Bake for 10 minutes.

The Inn on the Green

*T*his landmark Southern Colonial home rests atop the hill overlooking the MaCalGrove Country Club. Each of the four guestrooms here is named after a Southern city and features garden decor, inspired by the gardens surrounding the inn and inviting summer guests to relax and enjoy the birds and butterflies.

The Jilek family — Brad and Shelley and their kids, Patrick and Kristina, along with miniature schnauzer Winston — welcome guests who come to stroll through the gardens, answer the challenge of the golf course, or identify the many birds that call the estate home. After a day biking on the Root River Trail, flyfishing the many trout streams or antiquing, or cross-country skiing, guests can relax in the poolroom and use the whirlpool or sauna.

Brad, an electrical contractor, will answer those building and remodeling questions. But to really get him talking, mention his Harley-Davidson or Z-3 Roadster. He has mapped out some of the greateest backroads in Minnesota's Bluff Country and will not only share his route, but will share his garage with guests driving special bikes and cars. Shelley, a former teacher, loves cooking and creative forms of sewing and needlework. She is happy to share recipes and has been featured in several cookbooks that are for sale at the Inn. Her evening desserts, which she serves in each guestroom, are legendary in Bluff Country. All the guestrooms have her handmade quilts, and guests awaken to the aroma of a gourmet breakfast. Learn more on the Web, www.bluffcountry.com/inngreen.htm

The Inn on the Green

Route 1, Box 205
Caledonia, MN 55921
507-724-2818
Fax 507-724-5571
Toll-free 800-445-9523

Pat's Oatmeal Bar Treats

"These were my son Pat's favorite cookies when he was growing up," recalled Innkeeper Shelley Jilek. "I first remember them as an after-school snack that my mother made when my sister and I were growing up." With oatmeal and peanut butter, these provide plenty of energy for travelers. Makes 30 bars.

⅔ cup shortening
1 cup brown sugar, packed
4 cups old-fashioned rolled or quick-cooking oats
1 teaspoon salt
½ cup light corn syrup
2 teaspoons vanilla extract

Frosting

1 package (6 ounces) semi-sweet chocolate chips
⅔ cup peanut butter

- Preheat oven to 400 degrees. Grease a 10 x 15-inch jelly roll pan.
- In a large bowl, mix together the shortening, brown sugar, oats, salt, corn syrup, and vanilla.
- Spread the mixture into pan. (You may wish to butter your hands and pat the mixture into the pan.) Bake for 10 minutes.
- To make the frosting, heat the chocolate chips and peanut butter in the microwave, stirring until smooth.
- Frost when bars are cool.

The Lamplighter
Bed & Breakfast

*J*udy and Heinz Bertram and their cocker spaniel, Freddy, welcome recreational and business travelers to their Queen Anne–style home, which was built in 1895 by a local doctor as his home and office. After living for more than twenty years in Germany and traveling extensively throughout Europe, the Bertrams brought their collection of fine antiques and original paintings and lithographs to their Michigan B&B.

They purchased their "dream B&B" virtually overnight, Judy said. She and Heinz added a deck with a gazebo and a red brick patio and extensive landscaping so that summer guests can enjoy refreshments outside. Judy is a Michigan native and former administrator in the Department of Defense school system overseas, and Heinz, originally from Germany, is a retired U.S. Air Force officer.

Breakfast may be served on the patio, in the gazebo, or in the formal dining room, depending on the season. Afterwards, guests might head off to swim in Lake Michigan, stroll along its miles of sandy beaches, walk to the lighthouse at the entrance to Ludington harbor, or shop for antiques. Guests find plenty of outdoor activities year 'round, including biking through Ludington State Park, rated one of the state's best, skiing on miles of groomed cross-country trails, or hiking or strolling along nature trails. Judy and Heinz are happy to help guests plan their itinerary to explore scenic Western Michigan. Learn more on the Web, www.laketolake.com/lamplighter

The Lamplighter

602 East Ludington Avenue
Ludington, MI 49431
616-843-9792
Fax 616-845-6070

Peanut Butter Chocolate Chip Cookies

When Innkeeper Heinz Bertram was growing up in Germany, he never heard of peanut butter or chocolate chips. "Now these cookies with this combination are among his favorites, and a hit with our guests," said Judy, his spouse. Makes 30 cookies.

½ cup sugar
⅓ cup brown sugar, packed
½ cup butter, softened
½ cup crunchy peanut butter
½ teaspoon vanilla extract
1 egg
1 cup flour
½ cup quick-cooking or old-fashioned rolled oats
1 teaspoon baking soda
¼ teaspoon salt
6 ounces semi-sweet chocolate chips

■ Preheat oven to 350 degrees.
■ With an electric mixer, beat together the sugar, brown sugar, butter, peanut butter, vanilla, and egg.
■ In another large bowl, stir together the flour, oats, baking soda, salt, and chocolate chips. Add to the sugar mixture and blend.
■ Drop the dough by teaspoonfuls onto an ungreased cookie sheet.
■ Bake for 10 to 12 minutes.

Birch Tree Inn Bed & Breakfast

*T*he Birch Tree Inn is perhaps best described as a Midwestern farmhouse in the heart of Flagstaff. Built by a contractor from Chicago in 1917, the two-story house has a large side-wrapped porch supported by Corinthian columns.

The home was owned by Joseph Waldhaus for 40 years, beginning in the late 1920s. Joe was a prominent member of the Flagstaff community, having served as a city council member, mayor and postmaster. Following his death in 1969, 22 members of the Sigma Tau Gamma Fraternity called 824 W. Birch their home for three years. In 1972, Sigma Chi took over residence with seven fraternity brothers. Thereafter, the house fell into some disrepair and went through a series of owners.

In 1988, it was the good fortune of Donna and Rodger Pettinger and Sandy and Ed Znetko, lifelong friends from Southern California, to purchase and refurbish the charming home and turn it into the Birch Tree Inn. The innkeepers have five guestrooms, each decorated in a different theme, using family heirlooms, momentoes and hand-made furniture. Downstairs, the living room is a good place to chat with other guests, who may be from any place in the world; the innkeepers have hosted guests from 35 different countries and 49 states. Guests might challenge each other to a game of ppool in the game room or tinkle the ivories on the piano, perhaps for an impromptu singalong.

Flagstaff is most well-known as the largest city closest to the south rim of the Grand Canyon. Visitors also find plenty of hiking, biking, antiquing, other shopping, and other in the area, including visiting Indian ruins or star gazing at the Lowell Observatory. Learn more on the Web, www.birchtreeinn.com

Birch Tree Inn Bed & Breakfast

824 W. Birch Avenue
Flagstaff, AZ 86001
Toll-free 888-774-1042
Fax 520-774-8462

Pineapple Raisin Drops

"My husband's aunt, Hannah Wagner, was the official baker in the family for more than 75 years," said Innkeeper Sandy Znetko. "This recipe was part of the legacy she left in her famous recipe box." Makes approximately 3 dozen soft cookies.

½ cup golden raisins
¾ cup crushed pineapple, with juice
1 cup brown sugar, packed
½ cup butter, softened
1 egg
1 teaspoon vanilla extract
2 cups flour
1 teaspoon baking soda
1 teaspoon cinnamon
¾ cup pecans, chopped

- Preheat oven to 375 degrees. Lightly grease cookie sheets.
- In a small bowl, mix raisins and crushed pineapple.
- With an electric mixer, cream brown sugar, butter, egg, and vanilla until fluffy. Beat in raisin-pineapple mixture.
- In another bowl, combine flour, baking soda, and cinnamon. Beat into creamed mixture.
- Blend in pecans by hand. Drop soft dough by teaspoonfuls onto cookie sheets.
- Bake for 12 to 15 minutes or until lightly browned.

The Inn on Maple

*T*he Inn on Maple sits below the bluffs of Green Bay, midway up the Door Peninsula. Originally constructed in 1902 as a residence and meat market, the building changed hands many times before its 1983 renovation as an inn. The National Register of Historic Places lists it as one of the finest examples of commercial-residential stovewood buildings in Wisconsin.

Guests at The Inn on Maple enjoy privacy in quiet rooms furnished with antique beds. Breakfast is served on the sunny enclosed front porch or in the Gathering Room and may include fresh fruits, juice, homemade muffins or breads, and special entrées, such as stuffed French toasts, fluffy pancakes, and baked strattas and egg dishes.

Louise and Bill Robbins moved from their suburban Chicago hometown and purchased the Inn in the spring of 1995. They wanted to enjoy and share the beauty of Door County and, in particular, Sister Bay. They have made it their goal to share their enthusiasm for the Door Peninsula with their guests all year 'round.

Sister Bay and the Door Peninsula offer dozens of activities in any season, from sledding, skiing, and snowmobiling to boating, biking, fishing, golfing, and swimming. The Inn is conveniently located near Peninsula State Park, Newport State Park, Birch Creek Music Center, nature sanctuaries, the village beach, restaurants, shops, and a bluffside hiking trail.

The Inn on Maple
414 Maple Drive
Sister Bay, WI 54234
920-854-5107

Potato Chip Cookies

Never know what to do with the crumbles of potato chips left at the end of the bag? Well, take lemons and make lemonade ... er ... ah ... cookies! "This light, melt-in-your-mouth cookie has been a favorite of ours for years," said Innkeeper Louise Robbins. Makes 24 cookies.

    1   cup butter or margarine
    ½   cup sugar
    1   teaspoon vanilla extract
    1¾ cups flour, sifted
    ¾   cup crushed potato chips
        powdered sugar

- Preheat oven to 350 degrees.
- With an electric mixer, cream the butter, sugar, and vanilla extract. Beat in flour and potato chips.
- Roll dough into 1½-inch balls and place on an ungreased cookie sheet.
- Bake for 15 minutes or until lightly brown.
- Remove from oven and while still hot, dust with powdered sugar.
- Let cool and dust with powdered sugar again.

Cleburne House

*T*his beautifully restored Queen Anne-style Victorian was built in 1886. Vestiges of its heritage are evident its twelve-foot ceilings, massive pocket doors, stained glass windows, and wraparound veranda with gingerbread trim. Innkeeper Jan Bills, who searched high and low across Texas before discovering this Victorian home, has filled the house with her antique doll and furniture collection.

The four guestrooms are located on the second floor, and two of them have access to a screened porch.. Jan completely redecorated the house in 1997 with new wallpaper, paint and draperies. Because she loves to garden, she tilled all the garden surrounding the house to recondition the soil for beautiful flowers. The Inn has been the site of many weddings over the past two years.

Cleburne House's magnificent gardens contain crepe myrtle, Carolina jasmine, large oaks, flower shrubs, herbs, and roses. Visitors linger on the wide veranda, enjoying tea and homemade cookies and ice cream and watching wild birds and hummingbirds flit among nearby feeders.

Cleburne House is within walking distance of the historic Johnson County Courthouse, Andrew Carnegie Library, Layland Museum, and many interesting antique shops. Also nearby are golf courses, canoeing, boutiques, Pat Cleburne State Park, and Texas Wildlife Safari. After a busy day, guests love to relax in the front parlor, where they're welcome to play Jan's grandmother's piano, read, or play board games. Learn more on the Web, www.digitex.net/cleburnehouse/

Cleburne House
201 N. Anglin
Cleburne, TX 76031
817-641-0085

Pride of Iowa Cookies

"My sister, Carol DeLong, gave this cookie recipe to me years ago," said Innkeeper Jan Bills. *"These cookies are hearty and robust and full of healthy foods."* Makes 36 cookies.

½ cup shortening
½ cup butter or margarine
1 cup brown sugar, packed
1 cup sugar
2 eggs
½ teaspoon vanilla extract
2½ cups flour
¼ teaspoon salt
½ teaspoon baking soda
½ cup coconut
2 cups old-fashioned rolled oats
1 cup corn flakes
½ cup chopped nuts

- Preheat oven to 350 degrees. Grease cookie sheets.
- With an electric mixer, cream the shortening, butter, brown sugar, and sugar.
- Add eggs and vanilla and beat until light and creamy.
- Beat in the flour, salt, baking soda, coconut, oats, corn flakes, and nuts; mix well, by hand, if necessary.
- Drop the dough by teaspoonfuls onto cookie sheets.
- Bake for 15 minutes or until browned.

Madelyn's in the Grove

*U*nion Grove is a small farming community at the center of seven counties, in the heart of North Carolina music country. Madelyn and John Hill, proprietors of Madelyn's in the Grove, call this area in northern Iredell County "a little piece of heaven."

Madelyn's in the Grove offers guests easy access to a wealth of musical events year round, including the annual Old Time Fiddler's Convention, the Merle Watson Festival, and a nearby "pickin' and singin'" each week. The Hills offer a variety of special weekend packages that cater to other interests as well: an Antique Getaway (including coupons, a picnic lunch, and a map to antique shops within fifty miles), a Watercolor Getaway (with artist-led classes), the popular "How to Attract Birds to Your Yard" weekend (featuring lessons in bird identification and a morning bird count), and Murder Mystery weekends.

A day at Madelyn's in the Grove begins with a hearty gourmet breakfast, and ends with cheese and crackers, sweets, lemonade, and tea. Five unique guestrooms, cheerily decorated, promise a peaceful slumber.

Madelyn's in the Grove
P.O. Box 298
1836 West Memorial Highway
Union Grove, NC 28689
704-539-4151
800-948-4473
Fax 704-539-4080

Quick Cinnamon Coffee Bars

The aroma of cinnamon while these bars are baking makes you want to eat them warm, from the oven. Madelyn Hill, innkeeper, loves them with the first cup of coffee in the morning, and that's why they're named "coffee bars." Makes 16 bars.

$\frac{1}{2}$ cup butter
$\frac{1}{2}$ cup sugar
  1 egg, beaten
  1 teaspoon vanilla extract
  1 cup flour
$\frac{1}{3}$ cup sugar
  1 teaspoon cinnamon
  1 cup finely chopped pecans

- Preheat oven to 350 degrees. Liberally grease an 8 x 11-inch pan.
- With an electric mixer, cream the butter and $\frac{1}{2}$ cup sugar.
- Beat in the egg and vanilla; mix well. Beat in the flour.
- Spread into pan.
- In a small bowl, combine $\frac{1}{3}$ cup sugar with cinnamon and nuts. Sprinkle over the dough. Press cinnamon mixture down into dough with your hands.
- Bake for 25 to 30 minutes. Cut while warm. "These bars freeze beautifully."

Linden Lea on Long Lake

*J*im and Vicky McDonnell took a deteriorating summer cottage and turned it into a contemporary, multilevel B&B with two guestrooms, both with window seats from which to watch the sunset. Guests at this lakeside B&B can work up quite an appetite. They are welcome to swim on the inn's Long Lake beach, fish, or take the rowboat over to one of the islands. After a busy day, visitors are happy to curl up by the fire, where they admire the inn's lovely, solid cherry mantel, hand carved in 1880.

Linden Lea takes its name from the Lake District in England. Long Lake was referred to by Native Americans as the Lake of Many Islands. Multilevel sundecks take guests through the birch trees and ferns to the beach.

The B&B is located minutes from Traverse City, Interlochen Center for the Arts, the Sleeping Bear Dunes National Lakeshore, and other area attractions. Guests come year 'round to enjoy the many Lake Michigan attractions and special packages Vicky has created, such as cooking classes. E-mail address is lindenlea@aol.com

Linden Lea on Long Lake
279 South Long Lake Road
Traverse City, MI 49684
616-943-9182

Raspberry Almond Bars

Innkeeper Vicky McDonnell impresses guests with these bars, which really aren't that hard to make. They disappear fast, however! Makes 9 bars.

1 **cup butter**
1 **cup sugar**
1 **egg**
1 **teaspoon almond extract**
2½ **cups flour**
½ **teaspoon baking powder**
¼ **teaspoon salt**
   raspberry jelly

■ Preheat oven to 350 degrees.
■ With an electric mixer, cream butter and sugar. Beat in egg and almond extract.
■ Mix in flour, baking powder, and salt.
■ Spread mixture into a 9-inch square baking dish. Smooth surface with a wet fork.
■ Drag a wooden spoon handle through the dough, no bigger than ½–inch deep and ½–inch wide, "mostly to contain the jelly so it doesn't spread all over creation and back!" Fill the little trenches with raspberry jelly.
■ Bake for 15 minutes. Cool before cutting.

Wedgwood Inns

*W*hen Carl Glassman and Dinie Silnutzer-Glassman decided to make career changes, they did their research, worked in the hospitality industry, and then threw caution to the wind. A nineteenth-century home came up for sale, one that Carl had noticed for quite some time, and they started in on the major restoration needed.

The resulting Wedgwood House, named after their collection of china, opened in 1982, just a few blocks from the village center of this historic Bucks County river town. But that was just the beginning — it turned out they enjoyed innkeeping so much, they restored other inns, and now teach classes to aspiring innkeepers, as well.

Their bed and breakfasts are nineteenth-century homes on more than two acres of landscaped grounds. Guests can enjoy the gardens, gazebo, and a game of croquet, played in traditional costume, at tea-time in the summer. In the winter, tea and treats are enjoyed fireside in the parlor.

Dinie and Carl offer fresh-baked pastries, warm comforters, a glass of homemade almond liqueur before bed, and other touches to make guests comfortable. They host a number of special events, including historic re-enactments, romantic getaways, relaxation retreats, and other events created purely for guests' enjoyment. Learn more about the inns on the Web, www.new-hope-inn.com

Wedgwood Inns
111 West Bridge Street
New Hope, PA 18938
215-862-2520
Fax 215-862-2570

Raspberry Swirl Brownies

"This brownie recipe looks as good as it tastes," said Innkeeper Carl Glassman. The combination of chocolate and raspberry will satisfy even the most particular sweet tooth or brownie expert. Makes 16 to 20 brownies.

     4 ounces semi-sweet chocolate
     ¾ cup butter
     2 cups sugar
     1 tablespoon water, milk or buttermilk
     3 eggs
     1 teaspoon vanilla extract
     1 cup flour
     ½ teaspoon baking soda
     ¼ teaspoon salt
     1 cup chopped pecans
     1 cup mini semi-sweet chocolate chips
     ½ cup seedless raspberry jam

- Preheat oven to 350 degrees. Spray a 9 x 13-inch pan with non-stick cooking spray.
- In a large microwave safe bowl, place the semi-sweet chocolate and butter. Microwave on medium-high, stirring every 30 seconds or so until chocolate aand butter are melted and smooth.
- With an electric mixer, beat the chocolated, butter, sugar and water or milk until smooth and cool.
- Add the eggs to the mixture, one by one, beating after each.
- Beatt in the vanilla, flour, baking soda, and salt. Stir in the pecans and mini chips.
- Turn the batter into pan and spread to the sides. Stir the raspberry jam to "loosen" it. Top brownie batter with jam and swirl the jam in with a knife.
- Bake for 40 to 45 minutes or until a toothpick inserted in the center comes out clean.

Yankee Hill Inn Bed & Breakfast

The ambiance of quiet, small town life in the heart of the Kettle Moraine recreational area is what Yankee Hill Inn Bed and Breakfast Innkeepers Peg and Jim Stahlman find draws guests to their two historic homes-turned-B&Bs.

Yankee Hill Inn B&B is comprised of two historic homes restored by the Stahlmans. One is a Sheboygan County landmark, a Queen Anne Victorian–style, built in 1891. The other is an 1870 Gothic Italianate listed on the National Register of Historic Places. Both were built in the "Yankee Hill" area of Plymouth by hard-working, affluent brothers, Henry and Gilbert Huson.

Yankee Hill Inn has 12 guestrooms, decorated with period antiques and other touches to reflect historic lodging. Six guestrooms have single whirlpool tubs. Land-scaped yards, parlors, fireplaces, and an enclosed front porch allow the guests to gather and relax. Each morning, guests wake up to the aroma of a full breakfast, featuring home-baked muffins and breads, and the cookie jar is open to guests.

From the Inn, guests take a short walk through Huson Park and across the Mullet River footbridge into downtown Plymouth, where they can explore charming antique and gift shops and dine in excellent restaurants. At the Plymouth Center is an art gallery, the Plymouth Historical Museum, and visitor information.

Outdoor adventures surround Plymouth in the glacially sculpted terrain. Enjoy the Kettle Moraine State Forest, many lakes, marked nature trails and the Ice Age Trail for hiking and biking. The paved Old Plank Road recreational trail, historic Plymouth walking tour, Road America race track and the Kohler Design Center, featuring the latest in Kohler bathroom and kitchen ideas, are also popular. Sheboygan and Lake Michigan are just 15 minutes away. Learn more on the Web, www.yankeehillinn.com

Yankee Hill Inn Bed & Breakfast
405 Collins Street
Plymouth, WI 53073
920-892-2222 ■ Fax 920-892-6228

Swiss Meringue Bars

"These bars have been one of the Stahlman family favorites long before innkeeping days — and we've been in this career for 11 years!" Peg Stahlman loves the chewy bottom layer with chocolate chips and nuts, making a wonderful base for the brown-sugared meringue top. Makes 24 bars.

  1 cup margarine (half butter may be used)
½ cup sugar
½ cup brown sugar, packed
  2 eggs, separated
  1 tablespoon water
  2 cups flour
  1 teaspoon baking powder
½ teaspoon baking soda
¼ teaspoon salt
½ cup semi-sweet chocolate chips
  1 cup chopped nuts
  1 cup brown sugar, packed

- Preheat oven to 350 degrees.
- With an electric mixer, cream margarine, sugar, and ½ cup brown sugar. Add egg yolks and water, and mix well.
- In another bowl, sift together flour, baking powder, baking soda, and salt. Add to butter mixture and mix well.
- Press mixture into a 9 x 13-inch baking pan. Sprinkle with chocolate chips and nuts.
- Beat egg whites until stiff, gradually adding 1 cup brown sugar.
- Drop meringue by spoonfuls and spread on top of chocolate chips and nuts.
- Bake for 30 to 35 minutes. Cool before cutting into bars.

Wedgwood Inns

*W*hen Carl Glassman and Dinie Silnutzer-Glassman decided to make career changes, they did their research, worked in the hospitality industry, and then threw caution to the wind. A nineteenth-century home came up for sale, one that Carl had noticed for quite some time, and they started in on the major restoration needed.

The resulting Wedgwood House, named after their collection of china, opened in 1982, just a few blocks from the village center of this historic Bucks County river town. But that was just the beginning — it turned out they enjoyed innkeeping so much, they restored other inns, and now teach classes to aspiring innkeepers, as well.

Their bed and breakfasts are nineteenth-century homes on more than two acres of landscaped grounds. Guests can enjoy the gardens, gazebo, and a game of croquet, played in traditional costume, at tea-time in the summer. In the winter, tea and treats are enjoyed fireside in the parlor.

Dinie and Carl offer fresh-baked pastries, warm comforters, a glass of homemade almond liqueur before bed, and other touches to make guests comfortable. They host a number of special events, including historic re-enactments, romantic getaways, relaxation retreats, and other events created purely for guests' enjoyment. Learn more about the inns on the Web, www.new-hope-inn.com

Wedgwood Inns
111 West Bridge Street
New Hope, PA 18938
215-862-2520
Fax 215-862-2570

Thumbprint Cookies

"Our young daughter, Jessica, 'Innkeeper Apprentice Extraordinaire,' especially likes to assist us in preparing this cookie recipe," said Innkeeper Extraordinaire Carl Glassman. Guess which part Jessica likes best? (Wrong - it's eating them!) Makes 4 dozen cookies.

- 1 cup butter or margarine, softened
- ¾ cup sugar
- 2 eggs, separated
- 1 teaspoon almond or vanilla extract
- 2 cups flour
- ¼ teaspoon salt
- 1¼ teaspoons cinnamon, optional
- ¼ cup chopped nuts, optional
  plum jelly or jam

- With an electric mixer, beat the butter at medium speed until creamy.
- Add the sugar and beat well.
- Add the egg yolks and almond or vanilla extract. Beat again.
- Stirring by hand to blend, add the flour, salt, and cinnamon.
- Cover the bowl with plastic wrap and let the mixture chill in the refrigerator for about an hour.
- Preheat oven to 350 degrees. Grease cookie sheets.
- Roll the dough into balls the size of a quarter. If using the nuts, whip the egg whites slightly with a fork, dip the balls in the egg whites, and then roll in the chopped nuts.
- Place the cookies 2 inches apart on cookie sheets.
- Press a thumb or spoon deep into each dough ball to make a "well" or thumbprint in the center.
- Bake for 12 to 15 minutes, or until cookies are lightly browned around the edges.
- Transfer the sheet to a cooling rack. While cookies are cooling, spoon ¼ teaspoon of jelly or jam into each thumbprint.

The Inn at Merridun

*M*erridun, an antebellum mansion listed on the National Register of Historic Places, is one of the most regal homes in upstate South Carolina. The mansion was built in 1855–57 in the Georgian style by William Keenan, a local merchant and a mayor of Union. In 1876, the house and property were acquired by Benjamin C. Rice, a local lawyer, who inherited a plantation that adjoined the Keenan property. With the new purchase, the estate covered 8,000 acres and grew cotton. Major renovations were made to the home in the early 1900s. Eventually, Rice's grandson, T.C. Duncan, inherited the house and renamed it "Merridun," a combination of three family names, Merriman, Rice, and Duncan. In 1893, Duncan almost single-handedly restored Union to its former position of wealth and prestige by introducing the textile industry to the city. He built the first successful cotton mill within sight of this mansion. Duncan replaced this home's original Doric columns with Corinthian columns, and he added marble porticos on the side wings, resulting in more than 2,400 square feet of porch space alone.

The 7,900-square-foot inn features a curved staircase, 14-foot ceilings with crystal chandeliers, a music room, large foyers on both floors, five bedrooms, and a third-story cupola. Despite its overwhelming size, Innkeepers Jim and Peggy Waller have made the mansion cozy and inviting. After retiring from long Navy careers, Peggy and Jim acquired the mansion, now sitting on nine acres, from T.C. Duncan's descendants. Today they offer five guestrooms to guests who come to enjoy the tranquillity of another era amid the shady oaks and magnolias. They welcome guests with J.D., the inn's cat, who was featured in "Southern Living" Magazine (his innkeeping skills are almost purr-fect). Learn more on the Web, www.bboonline.com/sc/merridun/

The Inn at Merridun
100 Merridun Place
Union, SC 29379
864-427-7052 ■ Fax 864-429-0373

Tropical Jewels

Refreshing and crunchy, with a taste of coconut and rum. "Change the flavor of the preserves to give new colors and tastes," advises Innkeeper Peggy Waller. "And please use fresh nutmeg — the difference in flavor is indescribable!" Makes 50 to 60 small cookies.

> 1 cup butter, softened (or ½ cup margarine and ½ cup butter)
> ¾ cup sugar
> 1 cup coconut
> ½ teaspoon rum extract
> 2½ cups flour
> ¼ teaspoon salt
> ¼ teaspoon freshly grated nutmeg
> variety of jams for filling

- Preheat oven to 350 degrees.
- Cream the butter and sugar until fluffy. Add the coconut and rum extract.
- Add the flour, salt, and nutmeg, and blend until just smooth. Refrigerate the dough for 30 minutes.
- Place tablespoonsful of dough onto an ungreased cookie sheet. Make a small indentation in the top of each cookie. Fill the indentation with about ¼ to ½ teaspoon of jam or preserves.
- Bake for about 15 minutes or until the edges of the cookies are light brown. Cool on racks. To store, keep tightly covered.

Inn at Cedar Crossing

*A*t the Inn at Cedar Crossing, Innkeeper Terry Smith's guests are treated to a hearty continental breakfast that includes a number of wonderful creations by the Inn's pastry chef.

This Historic Register mercantile building was erected in 1884, with shops at street level and merchant's quarters upstairs. In 1985, Terry, a banker who was active in local historic preservation, purchased the building to remake into an inn. After extensive restoration, the upstairs was transformed into an inviting inn, and, later, the street level became an acclaimed restaurant with Victorian era decor.

Today, the inn has nine guestrooms with period antiques, custom-crafted poster and canopied beds, and elegant decor. Many of the guestrooms have fireplaces graced with antique mantels, double whirlpool tubs, private porches, and televisions and VCRs hidden in armoires. All of the rooms feature plump down-filled comforters and decorator fabrics, wallpapers, and linens. The Gathering Room is a relaxing spot for guests to gather by the fireplace and enjoy locally pressed apple cider, popcorn, and those homemade cookies fresh from the Inn's baking kitchen.

This Inn's restaurant has been named as one of the Top 25 restaurants in the state by the *Milwaukee Journal-Sentinel*. Open daily for all three meals, the restaurant specializes in fresh ingredients, enticingly prepared entrées, and sinful desserts, and a casual pub serves liquid refreshments. The Inn's guests head out to enjoy Door County's hiking, biking, antiquing, shopping, golfing, or just poking along the back roads of this scenic peninsula bordered by Lake Michigan. Learn more on the Web, www.innatcedarcrossing.com

Inn at Cedar Crossing

336 Louisiana Street
Sturgeon Bay, WI 54235
920-743-4200
Fax 920-743-4422

Turtle Bars

"We serve and sell these at our restaurant's bakery counter sometimes," said Innkeeper Terry Smith. "They are a huge hit!" She suggests keeping them chilled; otherwise, the chocolate on top gets soft and can make a melty mess. Makes 24 to 32 very rich bars.

1½ cups flour
½ teaspoon baking powder
¼ teaspoon salt
4 tablespoons butter, chilled
1 egg
½ teaspoon vanilla extract
1½ tablespoons ice water

Filling

1 cup butter
1 cup brown sugar, packed
3 cups coarsely chopped pecans
¼ cup heavy (whipping) cream

Glaze

1 package (12 ounces) semi-sweet chocolate chips
½ cup butter

- Preheat the oven to 350 degrees. Grease a 9 x 13-inch baking pan.
- In food processor (or in large bowl, using pastry cutter), mix flour, baking powder, and salt.
- Cut in butter until mixture resembles cornmeal.
- In small bowl, combine egg, vanilla, and ice water. Add to dry mixture, mixing only until ingredients are barely incorporated and crumbly.
- Press crust mixture evenly into pan. Bake 5 minutes.
- Place butter and brown sugar in medium saucepan and bring to a boil, stirring frequently. Cook to soft ball stage (240 degrees on candy thermometer). Remove from heat.
- In a small bowl, combine pecans and cream. Stir into caramel mixture. Pour over baked crust and smooth out.
- Melt chocolate and butter in double boiler or microwave. Spread evenly over filling. Chill until set and cut into bars. Store chilled.

Fairlea Farm Bed & Breakfast

*G*uests at Fairlea Farm Bed & Breakfast enjoy a spectacular view of vast pastures and the Blue Ridge Mountains. "On a clear day, if you know exactly where to look, you can even see cars in the distance along Skyline Drive in Shenandoah National Park," said Innkeeper Susan Longyear.

Fairlea Farm is a working sheep and cattle farm within two blocks of the center of the historic village of Little Washington, Virginia. George Washington surveyed and laid out plans for the village when he was 17 years old, note the Longyears. Susan and Walt opened the fieldstone manor house as a four-guestroom inn in order to share the peacefulness of the farm life with travelers.

In addition to Shenandoah National Park, plenty of attractions and activities can keep guests as busy as they like to be. Nearby are craft and antique shops, art galleries, vineyards and wineries, and Civil War battlefields. Those who love outdoor activities can visit Luray Caverns, hike, ride horses, golf, and fish close by. Learn more on the Web, www.bnb-n-va.com/fairlea.htm

Fairlea Farm Bed & Breakfast
P.O. Box 124
636 Mt. Salem Avenue
Washington, VA 22747
540-675-3679
Fax 540-675-1064

Virginia Peanut Butter Cookies

These cookies are often on hand to be served as a treat with fresh apple cider, ice cold or steaming hot. Makes approximately 5 dozen cookies.

- 1 cup margarine (not butter)
- 1 cup Virginia peanut butter, creamy or chunky
- 1 cup dark brown sugar, packed
- 1 cup sugar
- 2 eggs
- 1 teaspoon vanilla extract
- 2½ cups flour
- 1 teaspoon baking powder
- 1 teaspoon baking soda
- ¼ teaspoon salt
- additional sugar

- Preheat the oven to 350 degrees.
- With an electric mixer, beat together the margarine and peanut butter. Add the brown sugar and sugar and beat until blended. Beat in the eggs and vanilla.
- In another bowl, combine the flour, baking powder, baking soda, and salt. Add to the peanut butter mixture and beat well.
- Make 1-inch balls of dough (dough may need to be refrigerated for about 30 minutes at this point for ease in handling).
- Roll the balls in a small dish of sugar and place about 1 inch apart on an ungreased cookie sheet.
- With a fork slightly moistened in water, press a criss-cross pattern on each cookie ball.
- Bake for 11 to 13 minutes, or until lightly browned. Cool on a wire rack.

ARIZONA
Birch Tree Inn Bed & Breakfast; Flagstaff, AZ — *Cashew Drop Cookies (19),*
Pineapple Raisin Drops (107)
The Graham Bed & Breakfast Inn and Adobe Village; Sedona, AZ —
Chocolate Chip Oatmeal Cookies (25)
White Mountain Lodge; Greer, AZ — *Orange-Spice Snickerdoodles (99)*

CALIFORNIA
Lord Mayor's Bed & Breakfast Inn; Long Beach, CA — *Hazelnut Squares (61), Molasses*
Applesauce Cookies (77), Molasses Planks (79)
The Gosby House; Pacific Grove, CA — *Fudge Mound Cookies (55)*

FLORIDA
Thurston House; Maitland, FL — *Grandma Webber's Gingersnaps (59), Hermit Bars (63)*

MAINE
Old Iron Inn Bed & Breakfast; Caribou, ME — *Caramel Walnut Bars (17),*
Little Lime Bites (71)

MASSACHUSETTS
Isaiah Hall Bed & Breakfast Inn; Dennis, MA — *Old-Fashioned Peanut Butter Cookies (93)*

MICHIGAN
Linden Lea on Long Lake; Traverse City, MI — *Linden Scotch-a-Roo Bars (69), Raspberry*
Almond Bars (115)
The Lamplighter Bed & Breakfast; Ludington, MI — *No-Bake Chocolate Oatmeal Cookies*
(85), Peanut Butter Chocolate Chip Cookies (105)

MINNESOTA
Martin Oaks Bed & Breakfast; Dundas, MN — *Brandy Snaps (13)*
The Inn on the Green; Caledonia, MN — *Chocolate Drop Cookies (35),*
Pat's Oatmeal Bar Treats (101)
The Stone Hearth Inn; Little Marais, MN — *Grandma Catherine's Date Pinwheels (57)*
Thorwood and Rosewood Inns; Hastings, MN — *Ann's Famous Chocolate Chip Cookies*
(7), Chocolate Chip Shortbread (27), Double Almond Journey Cakes (49),
Maggie Lee's Sugar Cookies (73)

MISSOURI
The Doanleigh Inn; Kansas City, MO — *Chocolate Decadence Cookies (31), Chocolate*
Raspberry Streusel Squares (41)

NEW HAMPSHIRE
Apple Gate Bed & Breakfast; Peterborough, NH — *Apple Harvest Cookies (9),*
Crescent Cookies (45)
The Inn at Maplewood Farm; Hillsborough, NH — *Chocolate Pecan Butterscotch*
Shortbread (39)
Watch Hill Bed & Breakfast; Center Harbor, NH — *Center Harbor Firehouse Brownies (23),*
Chocolate Madeleines (37), Mom's Chocolate Meringue Cookies (81)

NEW MEXICO
Inn on the Rio; Taos, NM — *Chocolate Clouds (29), Favorite Decadence Layer Bars (51), Mexican Wedding Cakes (75)*

NORTH CAROLINA
Madelyn's in the Grove; Union Grove, NC — *Quick Cinnamon Coffee Bars (113)*

OREGON
McKenzie View Bed & Breakfast; Springfield, OR — *Orange-Cranberry Oatmeal Cookies (97)*
The Woods House Bed & Breakfast; Ashland, OR — *Banana Lemon Bars with Chocolate Chips (11)*

PENNSYLVANIA
Rose Manor Bed & Breakfast; Manheim, PA — *Chocolate-Dipped Oatmeal Shortbread (33)*
Wedgwood Inns; New Hope, PA — *Raspberry Swirl Brownies (117), Thumbprint Cookies (121)*

SOUTH CAROLINA
The Inn at Merridun; Union, SC — *Tropical Jewels (123)*

TEXAS
Cleburne House; Cleburne, TX — *Pride of Iowa Cookies (111)*
The Delforge Place; Fredericksburg, TX — *Fruit Jam Meringue Bars (53)*
The Settlement at Round Top; Round Top, TX — *Mom's Norwegian Spritz Cookies (83)*

UTAH
The Old Miners' Lodge; Park City, UT — *Oatmeal Cookies (87)*

VIRGINIA
Fairlea Farm Bed & Breakfast; Washington, VA — *Virginia Peanut Butter Cookies (127)*

WASHINGTON
Island Escape Bed & Breakfast; Fox Island, WA — *Island Fruit Bars (65), Johnny Appleseed Cookies (67)*
Salisbury House; Seattle, WA — *Cathy's Cream Cheese Sugar Cookies (21)*
White Swan Guest House; Mt. Vernon, WA — *Old-Fashioned Chocolate Chip Cookies (91)*

WISCONSIN
Inn at Cedar Crossing; Sturgeon Bay, WI — *Turtle Bars (125)*
Justin Trails Country Inn; Sparta, WI — *Olga's Chewy Oatmeal Cookies (95)*
Lamb's Inn Bed & Breakfast; Richland Center, WI — *Coconut Oatmeal Cookies (43)*
The Inn on Maple; Sister Bay, WI — *Potato Chip Cookies (109)*
Yankee Hill Inn Bed & Breakfast; Plymouth, WI — *Oatmeal Jelly Bars (89), Swiss Meringue Bars (119), Crispy Skillet Cookies (47)*

WYOMING
Window on the Winds; Pinedale, WY — *Candy Cane Cookies (15)*

"Inn-dulge" Yourself and Your Friends with More B&B Cookbooks

Order additional copies of any of our popular B&B cookbook editions from your bookstore, gift shop, or by mail.

INNKEEPERS' BEST *is a series of collectible, single-theme cookbooks showcasing bed-and-breakfast innkeepers' most requested, "oh-so-good" recipes. Each 6 x 9–inch paperback retails for $9.95 ($12.95 each by 4th class mail; $13.95 each UPS ground service):*
- Innkeepers' Best *Muffins*
- Innkeepers' Best *Low-Fat Breakfasts*
- Innkeepers' Best *Cookies*
- Innkeepers' Best *Quick Breads*

WAKE UP & SMELL THE COFFEE *is a series of hefty 8 ½ x 11–inch softcover cookbooks packed with travel information, maps, an index, as well as more than ten chapters of breakfast, brunch, and other favorite fare from B&Bs in a particular region.*
- **Lake States Edition** *has 203 recipes from 125 B&Bs in Michigan, Wisconsin, and Minnesota: $15.95 ($18.95 by 4th class mail; $19.95 UPS ground service).*
- **Pacific Northwest Edition** *features more than 130 recipes from 58 B&Bs in Washington and Oregon: $11.95 ($14.95 each by 4th class mail, $15.95 each sent UPS).*
- **Northern New England Edition** *offers a delicious variety, from Banana Almond French Toast to Vermont Cheddar Pie. 171 recipes from 80+ B&Bs in Maine, Vermont, and New Hampshire: $14.95 ($17.95 by 4th class mail; $18.95 UPS ground).*

CHOCOLATE FOR BREAKFAST AND TEA *is our beautiful four-color, hardcover book, 7 x 7 inches, color photos, featuring 67 mouthwatering chocolate recipes from inns across the country. A fabulous gift — everyone knows someone who loves chocolate! $21.95 ($23.95 each by 4th class mail; $24.95 each UPS ground service)*

TO ORDER BY MAIL, send a check to Down to Earth Publications, 1032 W. Montana, St. Paul, MN 55117. Make checks payable to Down to Earth Publications. MN residents please add 7% sales tax. **TO ORDER WITH VISA OR MASTERCARD,** call us at 800-585-6211.

Mail to: Down to Earth Publications, 1032 W. Montana, St. Paul, MN 55117.

Please send me:

_____ Innkeepers' Best *Muffins*
_____ Innkeepers' Best *Low-Fat Breakfasts*
_____ Innkeepers' Best *Cookies*
_____ Innkeepers' Best *Quick Breads*
_____ WAKE UP & SMELL THE COFFEE — *Pacific Northwest Edition*
_____ WAKE UP & SMELL THE COFFEE — *Lake States Edition*
_____ WAKE UP & SMELL THE COFFEE — *Northern New England Edition*
_____ *Chocolate for Breakfast and Tea*

I have enclosed $_____ for _____ book(s). Send it/them to (no P.O. boxes for UPS):

Name: _____

Street: _____ Apt. No. _____

City: _____ State: _____ Zip: _____
(Please note: No P.O. Boxes for UPS delivery)